DO Drops

Volume 12

DO Drops
Volume 12

Daily Bible Devotional

Dr. Bo Wagner

Word of His Mouth Publishers
Mooresboro, NC

All Scripture quotations are taken from the **King James Version** of the Bible.

ISBN: 978-1-941039-45-8
Printed in the United States of America
©2024 Dr. Bo Wagner

Word of His Mouth Publishers
Mooresboro, NC
www.wordofhismouth.com

Cover art by Chip Nuhrah

Devotion 1

Bildad was now finished with his first screed against Job. He had reminded Job that God does not pervert judgment or justice. He had also gone on to say many things that were patently wrong when applied to Job. But now, as Job begins to answer him, he does so by actually stipulating to Bildad's view of God and justice:

Job 9:1 *Then Job answered and said, 2 I know it is so of a truth: but how should man be just with God? 3 If he* [God] *will contend with him* [man], *he* [man] *cannot answer him* [God] *one of a thousand.*

Job agreed that God did not pervert justice. On that much, he and Bildad agreed. But where they diverged was on whether a man, any man, could ever actually be considered "just" in God's eyes! Bildad clearly viewed himself as just and Job as unjust. What Job understood that Bildad did not, is that in and of himself, no man at all can ever be just in God's sight. If God were to lay a thousand accusations against any human being, that person could not answer back to a single one of them.

Job was thousands of years ahead of the curve on this one:

Romans 3:10 *As it is written, There is none righteous, no, not one:*

And this, friends, is why Christ had to die to begin with! Since even a perfect man like Job looked impure to a holy God, we know that all of us look utterly filthy to Him. And so, God sent His own perfect Son as a sacrifice for our sins so that we could be clothed in His righteousness.

If you are saved, whenever the devil reminds you of how dirty and filthy you are, DO think about

Job and remind the devil that Jesus died for you just as much as He did for Job!

Personal Notes:

_____

_____

_____

_____

_____

_____

_____

_____

_____

_____

_____

_____

_____

_____

_____

_____

_____

_____

_____

_____

_____

_____

_____

_____

_____

_____

_____

Devotion 2

As Job continues to answer Bildad, we come to a really unique and valuable portion of Scripture.

Job 9:5 *Which removeth the mountains, and they know not: which overturneth them in his anger.* **6** *Which shaketh the earth out of her place, and the pillars thereof tremble.* **7** *Which commandeth the sun, and it riseth not; and sealeth up the stars.* **8** *Which alone spreadeth out the heavens, and treadeth upon the waves of the sea.* **9** *Which maketh Arcturus, Orion, and Pleiades, and the chambers of the south.*

In verses five and six, Job spoke of the power of God as demonstrated in earthquakes. By the way, he was speaking figuratively and poetically when he spoke of the pillars of the earth trembling. He knew perfectly well the scientific truth about the earth, telling Bildad in Job 26:7 that God *"hangs the earth on nothing."*

In verse seven, he spoke of those days when there is such a heavy cloud cover that there is no sunrise to be seen and those same kind of nights when the stars also cannot be seen. Job clearly was an avid observer and student of nature.

But in verse nine, we come to the most fascinating portion, where Job mentioned three constellations by name: Arcturus (what we would call the Big Bear), Orion, and Pleiades (a group of stars in the Taurus constellation). He then mentioned *"the chambers of the South,"* which is a reference to the unseen regions of the southern hemisphere, with its own set of stars, as distinguished from those just mentioned of the northern. As Jamieson, Faussett, and Brown observed, "The true structure of the earth (the fact that it is a complete sphere, a ball) is here implied."

Don't tell the flat-earthers; that kind of thing could *ahem* "push them over the edge."

The constellations, nature of the universe, and design of earth were very well understood by ancient man. So when you read your Bible, DO realize that it was not written by human authors who were "ignorant people living in caves, trying to make fire." It was written by people every bit as smart as we are. On second thought, looking around at our world today, make that "people who were, in general, WAY smarter than us!"

Personal Notes:

_____

_____

_____

_____

_____

_____

_____

_____

_____

_____

_____

_____

_____

_____

_____

_____

Devotion 3

Job had spoken of the wonders of the universe, pointing, therefore, to the glory of the God who made it all. Now, he would bring that large truth home to a very small point.

Job 9:10 *Which doeth great things past finding out; yea, and wonders without number.* **11** *Lo, he goeth by me, and I see him not: he passeth on also, but I perceive him not.* **12** *Behold, he taketh away, who can hinder him? who will say unto him, What doest thou?* **13** *If God will not withdraw his anger, the proud helpers do stoop under him.* **14** *How much less shall I answer him, and choose out my words to reason with him?*

The general tenor of these words is, "God is so big and does such big things that I am too small for Him to bother with in my trials. He is angry with me for some reason, and my legs are not big enough to bear the weight He is piling on me. Since that is the case, how could I ever reason with Him even if I got the opportunity to do so?"

Those words break my heart because they show that Job understood God's bigness but had no clue about His smallness.

The God who made all of those constellations Job spoke of seconds earlier in verse nine would one day leave heaven itself, breeze right past all of them, and land in tiny Bethlehem, in poverty, in the tiny womb of an unknown virgin, live a life of anonymity, and then die like a common criminal.

And He would do all of it for us and for Job, who thought that God was too big to care about him.

When you praise God, DO praise Him for His bigness, but DO also praise Him for His magnificent smallness!

Personal Notes:

_____

_____

_____

_____

_____

_____

_____

_____

_____

_____

_____

_____

_____

_____

_____

_____

_____

_____

_____

_____

_____

_____

_____

_____

_____

Devotion 4

As Job continued speaking of the nature of God to Bildad, some of which he got right and some of which he got wrong, he finally got around to examining what he believed was the evidence of his assertions, evidence to be found in people and outcomes.

Job 9:22 *This is one thing, therefore I said it, He* [God] *destroyeth the perfect and the wicked.* **23** *If the scourge slay suddenly, he will laugh at the trial of the innocent.* **24** *The earth is given into the hand of the wicked: he covereth the faces of the judges thereof; if not, where, and who is he?*

This is an excellent example of gathering good data and yet arriving at bad conclusions. The data Job saw is very simply what we still see even today. Wicked men are generally in power, prosperous, and untroubled, while the righteous are generally abused and relegated to society's lower rungs. Many years later, David wrote an entire lengthy psalm about this very fact, Psalm 37.

But though Job got the effect right, he absolutely missed the cause and missed even worse on the conclusion. The devil and sinful man bring about evil, not God. And even when an evil man is in power, David observed in Psalm 37 that they one and all come to a very brutal end, while the righteous will never "end" at all!

This is something you need to come to grips with, or you will drive yourself crazy as you look at life and circumstances. So DO memorize this handy phrase: "There is a devil, but there's also a hell, and there is a God, so all will be well!"

Personal Notes:

_____

_____

_____

_____

_____

_____

_____

_____

_____

_____

_____

_____

_____

_____

_____

_____

_____

_____

_____

_____

_____

_____

_____

_____

_____

_____

_____

_____

Devotion 5

In Job's continued complaint, we once again find some very interesting insight into conditions in the ancient world.

Job 9:25 *Now my days are swifter than a post: they flee away, they see no good.* **26** *They are passed away as the swift ships: as the eagle that hasteth to the prey.*

When Job said, "*Now my days are swifter than a post: they flee away, they see no good,*" he was telling us again of his despair and how his days were quickly slipping away with no hope. But in telling us that, he used the illustration of them being "swifter than a post." A post was a runner, a deliverer of messages. "Post" office, anyone? The ancient world had a mail delivery system! We saw that very same thing in the book of Esther, where such posts were mentioned five times.

And then, in verse twenty-six, Job again referenced his despair and how his days were quickly slipping away with no hope, but this time, he used the illustration of swift ships. Early man was a sea-faring people and very good at it. We find that referenced in Jonah, in the accounts of Solomon's wealth, from the lips of Christ, and yes, even as early as Noah.

In that same verse, Job demonstrated his knowledge of nature once again, correctly identifying the eagle as a predator.

In other words, the chronological pride our generation shows, the belief that everyone before us was a bunch of ignorant rubes, is simply ludicrous.

DO have a high view of ancient man; they built the pyramids, and the best explanation our modern-day geniuses can come up with is, "Well, maybe aliens did it!"

Personal Notes:

_____

_____

_____

_____

_____

_____

_____

_____

_____

_____

_____

_____

_____

_____

_____

_____

_____

_____

_____

_____

_____

_____

_____

_____

_____

Devotion 6

As Job continued his complaint, he began to deal with the nature of God and righteousness.

Job 9:28 *I am afraid of all my sorrows, I know that thou wilt not hold me innocent.* **29** *If I be wicked, why then labour I in vain?* **30** *If I wash myself with snow water, and make my hands never so clean;* **31** *Yet shalt thou plunge me in the ditch, and mine own clothes shall abhor me.*

In verse twenty-eight, Job opined that he had every reason to fear and no reason to hope, for no matter what he did, God would not view him as innocent. And that belief led him to his assertion in verse twenty-nine that, since he would be viewed as wicked no matter what, there was no reason to even try to live right. He then expressed that exact same sentiment using another word picture, saying, "*If I wash myself with snow water, and make my hands never so clean; yet shalt thou plunge me in the ditch, and mine own clothes shall abhor me.*" That basically means, "If I do my best to wash and stay clean, your estimation of me will be 'he is so dirty, I may as well throw him into a ditch and wallow him around till even his clothes cannot stand to be on him.'"

And yet, God had said no such thing and had repeatedly called Job a perfect and an upright man.

Job did not sound like God, but he did sound a great deal like many preachers today, who, in their attempt to impress the holiness of God upon us, make it sound like we may as well just give up because God is angry and nit-picky and will always hold His nose and look at us in disgust.

That view is not supported by Scripture. Yes, God is holy enough to say, "*All our righteousnesses are as filthy rags*" (**Isaiah 64:6**), but He is also fair enough to acknowledge when we HAVE righteousnesses to look like anything!

Be careful not to make God out to be mean and unfair; DO recognize Him both for His holiness and for His even-handedness!

Personal Notes:

_____

_____

_____

_____

_____

_____

_____

_____

_____

_____

_____

_____

_____

_____

_____

_____

_____

_____

_____

_____

_____

_____

Devotion 7

There are moments, as we read the Scripture, that we could well wish to be able to shout back across the eons of time so that the people we are reading about could hear us. The next words from the trembling lips of Job give me one of those moments.

Job 9:32 *For he* [God] *is not a man, as I am, that I should answer him, and we should come together in judgment.* **33** *Neither is there any daysman betwixt us, that might lay his hand upon us both.*

That word that you see in verse thirty-three, daysman, occurs just this once in Scripture. It is, therefore, a very special word. In our modern vernacular, a daysman is a go-between, an arbitrator, one who grabs the hands of two opposing parties and bridges the gap.

Job believed that there was a holy, angry God out there who was very much opposed to him. He also believed that there was no one who could understand both sides of the conflict and ever act to bring them together. But before there ever was a Job, before there was ever even an earth for Job to live and suffer on, Revelation 13:8 tells us that there was a Lamb slain! Calvary had already been decided on before Calvary's Hill ever existed. Job's sins had already been predetermined to be laid on Christ before the devil ever laid an accusation of sin on Job. There was, at the very moment Job was mourning the non-existence of a daysman, a Daysman! Jesus, the second person of the Godhead, would become one hundred percent flesh so that He could be the perfect Daysman, the only one who could ever truly understand and bridge the gap between fleshly man and a holy God.

When you feel like no one really understands, DO smile and repeat these words, "There is a Daysman; His name is Jesus!"

Personal Notes:

_____

_____

_____

_____

_____

_____

_____

_____

_____

_____

_____

_____

_____

_____

_____

_____

_____

_____

_____

_____

_____

_____

Devotion 8

As Job continued his complaint into chapter ten, he let his emotions and agony guide his words, which hardly ever produce good results.

Job 10:1 *My soul is weary of my life; I will leave my complaint upon myself; I will speak in the bitterness of my soul.* **2** *I will say unto God, Do not condemn me; shew me wherefore thou contendest with me.* **3** *Is it good unto thee that thou shouldest oppress, that thou shouldest despise the work of thine hands, and shine upon the counsel of the wicked?*

Job was fine in saying, "*My soul is weary of my life.*" It was accurate and understandable. Even in asking God not to condemn him, he did not do too badly because it at least recognizes God's authority. Nor was asking God to show him why He was contending with him in any way disrespectful, even though it was inaccurate, since all of Job's problems came from Satan, not God. But when he got to verse three and said, "*Is it good unto thee that thou shouldest oppress, that thou shouldest despise the work of thine hands, and shine upon the counsel of the wicked?*" he completely blew it.

God did not oppress Job in the least. Every problem Job had came from the devil, and every blessing Job had came from God, and there were many, many of those blessings! God also did not "despise the work of His hands" in any of this; God set strict limits on what Satan could do, limits that allowed for God to eventually rebuild Job beyond anyone's wildest dreams. Nor did God "shine upon the counsel of the wicked;" later in the book, we will see Him making Job's mouthy friends come grovel to him.

One of the easiest mistakes in the world to make is speaking out of hurt. Pain makes a terrible guide, and words that are ill-spoken cannot be gotten back once we feel better. So before you speak from pain, DO consider letting some godly someone who is not in agony evaluate your words before you launch them out into the world!

Personal Notes:

_____

_____

_____

_____

_____

_____

_____

_____

_____

_____

_____

_____

_____

_____

_____

_____

_____

_____

_____

_____

_____

Devotion 9

The next few verses of Job's complaint make for an interesting study:

Job 10:4 *Hast thou eyes of flesh? or seest thou as man seeth? 5 Are thy days as the days of man? are thy years as man's days, 6 That thou enquirest after mine iniquity, and searchest after my sin?*

Flesh, man, man, man. These are the words Job attaches to God in verses four and five. He wanted to know if God had eyes of flesh or sees like a man sees. He wanted to know if God's days and years were like man's days. In other words, was God someone who had a very short lifespan? And what made him ask this was, according to verse seven, the fact that God was "enquiring after his iniquity and searching after his sin."

What Job was saying, in so many words, was, "God, you seem to be acting a whole lot like a human being. You seem to literally have nothing better to do than go through my life with a magnifying glass looking for reasons to hate on me."

Now, we know that Job was wrong in his view of God, but the thing that sticks out to me at the moment is how right he was in his view of man! As you are reading this right now, I bet you already have the name and face of someone bouncing around in your brain, some snoopy, overly pious, critical, miserable person who seems to have nothing better to do than actually go through everyone else's life and business looking for things wrong.

BlesS ThEIr HeaRts...

You cannot fix anyone else who is like this, so do not waste time trying. You can pray for God to help keep them preoccupied with other things, say, nuclear hemorrhoids, perhaps. But the main thing you can do is pray that you never become one of those people, so DO pray that prayer!

Personal Notes:

_____

_____

_____

_____

_____

_____

_____

_____

_____

_____

_____

_____

_____

_____

_____

_____

_____

_____

_____

_____

_____

_____

_____

_____

Devotion 10

Job's next words focused in on the hands of God, and there is much good and glory in those words.

Job 10:7 *Thou knowest that I am not wicked; and there is none that can deliver out of thine hand.* **8** *Thine hands have made me and fashioned me together round about; yet thou dost destroy me.* **9** *Remember, I beseech thee, that thou hast made me as the clay; and wilt thou bring me into dust again?* **10** *Hast thou not poured me out as milk, and curdled me like cheese?* **11** *Thou hast clothed me with skin and flesh, and hast fenced me with bones and sinews.* **12** *Thou hast granted me life and favour, and thy visitation hath preserved my spirit.*

Either stated or implied, Job believed and stated that God's hands are so strong that no one can deliver someone from them, physically made him, would bring him back to the dust he was formed from, had poured him out like milk and curdled him like cheese, had built his skeletal and musculature structure, had put the tendons and flesh upon all of that, and had preserved him to this point in his life.

Job did not get all of the details right; he was certainly wrong about God being the one who had "milk and cheesed" him. But Job was right about most of what he said, and he was certainly right about the fact that God's hands are very present and active hands in our lives!

The deist believes that God started the universe running and then took His hands off of it and is simply sitting back and watching as it unravels day by day.

No one would ever convince Job of that nonsense.

DO look at your hands. Now repeat this statement to get you ready for your day, "God's hands are way bigger than mine, and they are always active in my life and for my good!"

Personal Notes:

_____

_____

_____

_____

_____

_____

_____

_____

_____

_____

_____

_____

_____

_____

_____

_____

_____

_____

_____

_____

_____

_____

_____

Devotion 11

We will examine just one short verse in this devotion simply because it could be an entire book unto itself.

Job 10:15 *If I be wicked, woe unto me; and if I be righteous, yet will I not lift up my head. I am full of confusion; therefore see thou mine affliction;*

These words center around two "ifs" and two conclusions. Job said, "IF I be wicked, woe unto me. If I am bad, then I deserve all of these horrible things." Then he said, "IF I be righteous, yet will I not lift up my head. If I am good, I have no reason to be proud." But it seems to have quickly occurred to him that neither of those two possibilities had any way to explain his situation, let alone make it any better, because his next words were, "*I am full of confusion; therefore see thou mine affliction.*" In other words, "God, it occurs to me that I have no good answers here. I am not just a little bit confused; I am thoroughly confused. So, since listening to me ramble isn't likely to help, could you just please look at me instead?"

Job was confused, but one thing he grasped in his confusion was that when you cannot find "smart stuff to say" to God, it really isn't necessary anyway. Job knew that just having God see him sitting there on the ashes, covered in boils, not too far from ten fresh graves, would speak more eloquently than he ever could.

When you are confused, don't worry about coming up with the right words to say. DO instead just come before God and let Him see you!

Personal Notes:

_____

_____

_____

_____

_____

_____

_____

_____

_____

_____

_____

_____

_____

_____

_____

_____

_____

_____

_____

_____

_____

_____

_____

_____

_____

_____

_____

_____

_____

Devotion 12

As Job brought this round of his complaint to a close, he went back once again to his common refrain of longing for death.

Job 10:18 *Wherefore then hast thou brought me forth out of the womb? Oh that I had given up the ghost, and no eye had seen me!* **19** *I should have been as though I had not been; I should have been carried from the womb to the grave.* **20** *Are not my days few? cease then, and let me alone, that I may take comfort a little,* **21** *Before I go whence I shall not return, even to the land of darkness and the shadow of death;* **22** *A land of darkness, as darkness itself; and of the shadow of death, without any order, and where the light is as darkness.*

In verse twenty, Job asked God to "let him alone" so that he could have a little comfort before he dies. But it is his description of what would come next that is so intriguing. Job described it as a place he would not return from, a land of darkness and the shadow of death, a place without any order, a place so dark that even the light there would seem like darkness." What makes this so interesting is that it directly contradicts his view of the afterlife in moments where he spoke with a bit more faith, places like **Job 19:26** where he said, "A*nd though after my skin worms destroy this body, yet in my flesh shall I see God.*"

It seems that we are not the only ones capable of bouncing back and forth between mountain-high faith and bottom-of-the-sea despair. The key thing to remember, therefore, is to not make decisions like "should I live or die" in those moments when we are in the depths of despair! It was a very short trip for

Job from "There is no afterlife, and I want to die anyway" to "eternity is going to be so grand!" So if you want to make the right decisions, DO start by making decisions at the right times!

Personal Notes:

_____

_____

_____

_____

_____

_____

_____

_____

_____

_____

_____

_____

_____

_____

_____

_____

_____

_____

_____

_____

_____

_____

_____

_____

_____

Devotion 13

Job had heard from and answered Eliphaz and Bildad. But now the third Musketeer of Misery was going to stick his sword of a tongue into the mix.

Job 11:1 *Then answered Zophar the Naamathite, and said,* **2** *Should not the multitude of words be answered? and should a man full of talk be justified?* **3** *Should thy lies make men hold their peace? and when thou mockest, shall no man make thee ashamed?* **4** *For thou hast said, My doctrine is pure, and I am clean in thine eyes.* **5** *But oh that God would speak, and open his lips against thee;* **6** *And that he would shew thee the secrets of wisdom, that they are double to that which is! Know therefore that God exacteth of thee less than thine iniquity deserveth.*

It is almost hard to know where to start with Zophar. He takes Job's anguished words and tritely dismisses them as "words" and "talk" and "lies" and "mockery." He apparently had a first edition of Roget's Thesaurus and used/utilized/wielded/availed himself of it regularly. Then he wished that God would speak out loud AGAINST Job. Nothing like viewing God as your own pet pit bull, I suppose.

But worst of all was Zophar's assertion that "*God exacteth of thee less than thine iniquity deserveth.*" Let me remind you, Job had literally lost all ten of his children, all of his wealth, and all of his health. What exactly did Zophar want? Should God have resurrected Job's children and then allowed Job to suffer through having them die again?

I hope you know, "You are suffering badly, so you must be really wicked, so I wish you were hurting even worse than you are now!" is not exactly the right thing to say to anyone at a time like that, or any time, really. And Zophar was not speaking in positional terms, as in "All flesh is corrupt and deserving of hell," he and his friends laid serious practical accusations against Job, none of which were true.

It is interesting that God saw and stated the good in Job, and yet Zophar, in God's name, saw only evil in him, evil that was not even there to see. Believe it or not, it is okay to see the good in people. So DO see it, and if you cannot, DO at least consider keeping your mouth shut in case you are wrong!

Personal Notes:

_____

_____

_____

_____

_____

_____

_____

_____

_____

_____

_____

_____

_____

_____

_____

_____

_____

_____

_____

Devotion 14

Zophar, in continuing his assault on Job, decided to show himself to be "a man of solutions." After all, what good is pointing out a problem without also giving guidance on how to fix it?

Job 11:13 *If thou prepare thine heart, and stretch out thine hands toward him; **14** If iniquity be in thine hand, put it far away, and let not wickedness dwell in thy tabernacles. **15** For then shalt thou lift up thy face without spot; yea, thou shalt be stedfast, and shalt not fear: **16** Because thou shalt forget thy misery, and remember it as waters that pass away: **17** And thine age shall be clearer than the noonday; thou shalt shine forth, thou shalt be as the morning. **18** And thou shalt be secure, because there is hope; yea, thou shalt dig about thee, and thou shalt take thy rest in safety. **19** Also thou shalt lie down, and none shall make thee afraid; yea, many shall make suit unto thee.*

Zophar's solution in verse thirteen was for the man who worshipped God in the midst of tragedy (Job 1:20) to stretch out his hands to God. Zophar's solution in verse fourteen was for the man who constantly guarded against sin in his own family (Job 1:5) to put wickedness out of his tabernacles. In other words, if Job would just do all of the things he had already been doing, things that Zophar did not know he had already been doing because he did not bother to ask, everything would suddenly be all rainbows and unicorns for Job.

Zophar was a good example of a man who shows up late to a party and complains that no one brought the salsa, salsa that someone else bought the ingredients for, hand made, brought with them, and everyone already ate.

Not everything in life is going to make sense. Zophar viewed everything in the simplest possible terms, assuming everything is always somehow simple. But as long as there is a devil, there will be things that make no sense whatsoever. So when someone is facing disaster, DO consider the possibility that they may have done nothing whatsoever to cause or deserve it!

Personal Notes:

_____
_____
_____
_____
_____
_____
_____
_____
_____
_____
_____
_____
_____
_____
_____
_____
_____
_____
_____
_____
_____

Devotion 15

Would it surprise you if I told you that one of my very favorite Bible passages is found in the book of Job yet will never, EVER be found on a Hallmark card? Behold that passage, which begins Job's response to Zophar and his two friends.

Job 12:1 *And Job answered and said,* **2** *No doubt but ye are the people, and wisdom shall die with you.*

Are you sitting there reading those words and thinking, "Wait, Job sounds a bit sarcastic right there?"

Oh no, friend; he was not being "a bit" sarcastic. Those words are DRIPPING with sarcasm. Think Job with all ten fingers wiggling at the three attackers, lips pursed out, eyes wide, saying, "Oooooooooohhhhhhhh! You boys are soooooooooo smart! In fact, after you guys are gone, there won't be a single functioning brain cell left anywhere on earth. Wisdom is going to die when you do!"

That brings up a question, does it not? Is there actually a place for sarcasm in the daily life of believers, or should we always be kind and tender? Was Job wrong in what he did here? Let's look at both sides of the coin and see if we can figure it out. On the sarcasm side, Job used it here, Elijah used it in 1 Kings 18 when mocking the prophets of Baal, Jeremiah used it in Jeremiah 2 and 10 when discussing idols, Amos used it in Amos 4 against snooty women, even Jesus used it in Luke 15 when He spoke of people who "need no repentance." He also used it in lengthy, withering form against the Pharisees in Matthew 23.

And yet, on the other side, a soft answer turneth away wrath (Proverbs 15:1), and we are to let our speech be "alway with grace, seasoned with salt" (Colossians 4:6). So, is there even an answer to be found? Yes, there is: **Ecclesiastes 3:1** *To every thing there is a season, and a time to every purpose under the heaven.* There are times for sweetness, and there are times for sarcasm. And yet, precisely because our flesh is so prone to misuse barbed words, there are far more warnings against harsh words in the Bible than there are encouragements to them.

DO be willing to use sarcasm, if necessary, but DO also realize that it is not necessary nearly as often as our sinful flesh would like it to be!

Personal Notes:

_____

_____

_____

_____

_____

_____

_____

_____

_____

_____

_____

_____

_____

_____

_____

_____

_____

_____

Devotion 16

The problem that the three Musketeers of Misery had with Job was, in their view, a theological problem. But Job had a more accurate view of the real issue.

Job 12:5 *He that is ready to slip with his feet is as a lamp despised in the thought of him that is at ease.*

In the short parable Job just gave, he himself was the one ready to slip with his feet, and his three frienemies were the ones who were at ease. He pointed out that in such a circumstance, the one who is "on his last leg," as we would put it, is like a broken, useless lamp to those who are healthy and whole and unbattered by the circumstances of life.

We set up a time and place to meet together at a nice steakhouse. We drive our cars there, eat, fellowship, pay our way out, and go to our own comfortable homes. But then tragedy strikes, someone gets very sick, ends up losing a job, and even becomes homeless...

We would like to think that none of us would feel any differently about that person or family than we ever did. But are we sure that is the case? There is something in the heart of man that gets so very uncomfortable at the calamities of our peers. We tend to look for reasons, things they must have messed up, justifications to pull back from them.

We tend to be Zophars.

And yet Jesus did nothing wrong though He ended up on a cross. Paul did nothing wrong though he ended up in a prison. Stephen did nothing wrong though he was stoned to death. John did nothing wrong though he was exiled to Patmos.

DO make sure your friendships are not based on health and wealth; one day, you may be the one who has become poor and needy!

Personal Notes:

_____

_____

_____

_____

_____

_____

_____

_____

_____

_____

_____

_____

_____

_____

_____

_____

_____

_____

_____

_____

_____

_____

_____

_____

_____

Devotion 17

For all that he got right, Job himself still got much wrong as well. And in the next thing he said to Zophar, we find him going from good to bad to worse.

Job 12:6 *The tabernacles of robbers prosper, and they that provoke God are secure; into whose hand God bringeth abundantly.*

Job's point in saying these words was to counter the argument they kept making, namely that God had set up a divine order by which the righteous always prosper and the ungodly always suffer. And he was right to disagree with that faulty view of God. But all of that notwithstanding, notice the downward progression in verse six.

Good: Job was correct when he observed that the tabernacles of robbers prosper. Both Scripture and history show countless examples of that.

Bad: Job was incorrect when he observed that "*they that provoke God are secure.*" A more accurate statement would have been, "They that provoke God are secure – for now." Sinners may prosper for a while, but Judgment Day always comes.

Worse: Job was a million miles off base when he said of robbers, "*into whose hand God bringeth abundantly.*" Robbers may get rich, but it certainly isn't God loading their wagons!

Job was making the mistake most of us make, taking a very short-term view of the situation. But God never promised that things would be "right" all the way through the drama; He merely promised that all would be right by the time the curtain closes.

DO be patient; our entire life spans are just a few lines on God's master script!

Personal Notes:

_____

_____

_____

_____

_____

_____

_____

_____

_____

_____

_____

_____

_____

_____

_____

_____

_____

_____

_____

_____

_____

_____

_____

_____

_____

_____

_____

Devotion 18

Job is now going to make a second mistake as he counters Zophar, this one a mistake of extrapolation.

Job 12:6 *The tabernacles of robbers prosper, and they that provoke God are secure; into whose hand God bringeth abundantly. 7 But ask now the beasts, and they shall teach thee; and the fowls of the air, and they shall tell thee: 8 Or speak to the earth, and it shall teach thee: and the fishes of the sea shall declare unto thee. 9 Who knoweth not in all these that the hand of the LORD hath wrought this?*

Job's argument in these words is as follows. "God has set a system in place by which the unrighteous are more safe and secure than the righteous. And I know this because of what I see in nature. Big sharks eat little fish; lions eat gazelle; eagles eat doves. Might makes right; predators win."

The problem with Job's assertion is that man is not an animal.

Nature is indeed fallen and broken. All animal life was created to eat plants, but now they eat each other, and it is often a very gruesome thing. And yet, God created man alone in His image and deals with him as such. Man experiences things animals will never know of, things like divine chastisement and the guidance of the Holy Spirit, and the Judgment Seat of Christ where we will be rewarded or suffer loss based on our deeds.

Job had become something akin to a theological Darwinist, a proponent of the idea that God made a "survival of the fittest" world, even for mankind. And that is both an inaccurate and a miserable way to think and live.

DO remember that you are not an animal, and God has never and will never treat you as such!

Personal Notes:

_____

_____

_____

_____

_____

_____

_____

_____

_____

_____

_____

_____

_____

_____

_____

_____

_____

_____

_____

_____

_____

_____

_____

_____

_____

_____

Devotion 19

While Job's conclusions in his argument to Zophar may not always have been right, he did have a keen understanding of how big God is and how small man is. Look at the next few verses and notice the people that Job compares against God.

Job 12:16 *With him is strength and wisdom: the deceived and the deceiver are his. 17 He leadeth counsellors away spoiled, and maketh the judges fools. 18 He looseth the bond of kings, and girdeth their loins with a girdle. 19 He leadeth princes away spoiled, and overthroweth the mighty. 20 He removeth away the speech of the trusty, and taketh away the understanding of the aged. 21 He poureth contempt upon princes, and weakeneth the strength of the mighty. 22 He discovereth deep things out of darkness, and bringeth out to light the shadow of death. 23 He increaseth the nations, and destroyeth them: he enlargeth the nations, and straiteneth them again. 24 He taketh away the heart of the chief of the people of the earth, and causeth them to wander in a wilderness where there is no way. 25 They grope in the dark without light, and he maketh them to stagger like a drunken man.*

Job noted that God has power over the deceived, deceiver, counselors, judges, kings, princes (x2), mighty (x2), trusty, aged, nations, and chiefs. It's almost like He is the King of kings and Lord of lords!

Never allow yourself to have a very big view of humanity, and never allow yourself to have a small view of God. DO remember that He made us, not the other way around!

Personal Notes:

_____
_____
_____
_____
_____
_____
_____
_____
_____
_____
_____
_____
_____
_____
_____
_____
_____
_____
_____
_____
_____
_____
_____
_____
_____
_____
_____

Devotion 20

Job continued his response to Zophar into chapter thirteen. And as he did, he laid a couple of very cutting (and accurate) titles to his three adversaries.

Job 13:1 *Lo, mine eye hath seen all this, mine ear hath heard and understood it.* **2** *What ye know, the same do I know also: I am not inferior unto you.* **3** *Surely I would speak to the Almighty, and I desire to reason with God.* **4** *But ye are forgers of lies, ye are all physicians of no value.*

Forgers of lies and physicians of no value. Ouch.

Forgers or forged occurs only here and in Psalm 119:69. And in both cases, it means to smear. What a picturesque word! Job noted that his "friends" were making up lies and smearing him with them. And they very literally were; horrible, ugly lies.

Physicians of no value obviously means a medical practitioner who charges for their services, yet their services are utterly worthless. A quack. You know, like, totally hypothetically, if a doctor was world-famous yet destroyed lives and livelihoods all over the world proposing completely ridiculous "solutions" to a pandemic, changing his mind every other week, ignoring data he does not like, and making a fortune off of all of it.

Ahem.

Anyway, Job had an accurate view of his friends in this as well. They were seeing root causes that did not exist, proposing solutions that Job had always already been doing, not making anything any better, and yet smugly viewing themselves as better than him. They were "fixers" who made things more broken than they were before they arrived to help.

DO rehearse these words to yourself often, "I don't know everything." A person who grasps that one simple truth will not be as prone to "smear and quack" as those who do not!

Personal Notes:

_____

_____

_____

_____

_____

_____

_____

_____

_____

_____

_____

_____

_____

_____

_____

_____

_____

_____

_____

_____

Devotion 21

Job has now expanded his argument against Zophar to include Eliphaz and Bildad as well. And in the next few verses, he is going to lay a serious charge against them.

Job 13:5 *O that ye would altogether hold your peace! and it should be your wisdom.* **6** *Hear now my reasoning, and hearken to the pleadings of my lips.* **7** *Will ye speak wickedly for God? and talk deceitfully for him?* **8** *Will ye accept his person? will ye contend for God?* **9** *Is it good that he should search you out? or as one man mocketh another, do ye so mock him?* **10** *He will surely reprove you, if ye do secretly accept persons.*

Verse five is pretty biting, basically meaning, "If you would shut up, you would sound smarter." But in verses seven through nine, Job accuses his pious, spiritual-sounding attackers of being guilty of mocking God by what they are doing. They were putting words in God's mouth, words like "Job is wicked and horrible, and that is why I am judging him," words that contradicted what God Himself had actually said about Job.

But verse ten is the real stab to the heart. Job correctly surmised that, though they had not actually come out and said it, they believed that they were good and worthy of good, while Job was bad and worthy of bad. They had taken a "team us versus team Job" view of the situation, proudly believing that they were better than him and allowing their "theology" to be directed by that belief.

Any time our theology is based on how wonderful we are, it is a theology built on a cesspool.

DO view you and yours through the lens of right theology rather than viewing theology through the lens of you and yours!

Personal Notes:

_____

_____

_____

_____

_____

_____

_____

_____

_____

_____

_____

_____

_____

_____

_____

_____

_____

_____

_____

_____

_____

_____

_____

_____

_____

Devotion 22

Job was on a roll at this point, and he was about to produce one of the most glorious statements of faith in Scripture, born right out of a heated argument, of all places.

Job 13:11 *Shall not his excellency make you afraid? and his dread fall upon you?* **12** *Your remembrances are like unto ashes, your bodies to bodies of clay.* **13** *Hold your peace, let me alone, that I may speak, and let come on me what will.* **14** *Wherefore do I take my flesh in my teeth, and put my life in mine hand?* **15** *Though he slay me, yet will I trust in him: but I will maintain mine own ways before him.*

Job's three friends/accusers certainly were guilty of failing to fear God, as Job posited in verse thirteen. Fearing God brings humility not the pride and arrogance they were showing.

In verse fourteen, Job said, "*Wherefore do I take my flesh in my teeth, and put my life in mine hand?*" Adam Clarke correctly noted that this was "a proverbial expression; 'I risk everything on the justice of my cause. I put my life in my hand, I run all hazards; I am fearless of the consequences.'" In other words, Job was not going to back down. He knew the truth and was not going to be badgered out of it. If you have ever been in the right on something and yet been pressured from all sides to admit that you were wrong, you know what Job was feeling and facing here!

But it is in verse fifteen that Job utters the incomparable words, "*Though he slay me, yet will I trust in him: but I will maintain mine own ways before him.*"

Though He slay me, yet will I trust Him. That is the gold standard of faith! It is the Hebrew boys looking at Nebuchadnezzar and saying, "But if not, if He does not deliver us, we still won't bow to your idol." It is Stephen preaching Christ, knowing that one message will get him killed. It is faith that sees beyond time and into eternity.

DO make your faith a faith like this one, a faith with no reservations!

Personal Notes:

_____

_____

_____

_____

_____

_____

_____

_____

_____

_____

_____

_____

_____

_____

_____

_____

_____

_____

_____

_____

_____

Devotion 23

There will be a change of audience in Job's continued speech, and it will mark a dramatic point in the book. Job has just said, "Though He slay me, yet will I trust Him," and now he says the following:

Job 13:16 *He also shall be my salvation: for an hypocrite shall not come before him.* **17** *Hear diligently my speech, and my declaration with your ears.* **18** *Behold now, I have ordered my cause; I know that I shall be justified.* **19** *Who is he that will plead with me? for now, if I hold my tongue, I shall give up the ghost.* **20** *Only do not two things unto me: then will I not hide myself from thee.* **21** *Withdraw thine hand far from me: and let not thy dread make me afraid.* **22** *Then call thou, and I will answer: or let me speak, and answer thou me.*

In verses sixteen through nineteen, Job is addressing his three adversaries, and in verses twenty through twenty-two, he is speaking to God. In the first section, he assures those three mortals that he is, in fact, innocent and does not mind saying so; in fact, he would die rather than quietly agree to being guilty. In the second section, though, he asks God for certain terms of a meeting. He wants God to let up on the pressure and anguish so that he, Job, can stand and answer God in his full strength and with his full focus.

And if you are getting nervous about that part, you have good reason to. Job went far off the reservation on this one; no one, even on their best days, can stand calmly before God and contend with Him! Job would figure this out quickly later on in the book when God granted him the audience he sought.

Whether you are living right or living like the devil, never think for a moment that standing before

God will be anything other than awe-inspiring and maybe even terrifying. It is only by the blood of Jesus that we can call God our Abba, Father, not by any merit on our part. So DO approach God with reverence rather than a cocksure attitude!

Personal Notes:

_____

_____

_____

_____

_____

_____

_____

_____

_____

_____

_____

_____

_____

_____

_____

_____

_____

_____

_____

_____

_____

_____

_____

Devotion 24

As Job continued speaking to the God that he was not even sure was listening, he used quite a few words to say something that we normally take very few words to say.

Job 13:23 *How many are mine iniquities and sins? make me to know my transgression and my sin.* **24** *Wherefore hidest thou thy face, and holdest me for thine enemy?* **25** *Wilt thou break a leaf driven to and fro? and wilt thou pursue the dry stubble?* **26** *For thou writest bitter things against me, and makest me to possess the iniquities of my youth.*

Job used sixty words to say, "God, what have I done wrong?"

Have you ever been there? Have things ever fallen apart to such a degree that you were begging God to show you what sin you were being judged for so that you could repent of it and make the pain stop? In verse twenty-six, Job even guessed that it was some sin or sins from way back in the days of his youth that God was just now getting around to judging him for.

In reality, it is not the worst question in the world to ask. But it could be better. Job could have tried something like, "Lord, I don't want to assume anything since there is so much that I can never know. But if this calamity is, in fact, judgment for some sin that I have missed or forgotten about, I am trusting you to show me. And if you do, I will make it right."

We tell people all the time not to jump to conclusions about others. But maybe we need a reminder not to jump to conclusions about ourselves!

As much as is possible, DO give people the benefit of the doubt–even you!

Personal Notes:

_____

_____

_____

_____

_____

_____

_____

_____

_____

_____

_____

_____

_____

_____

_____

_____

_____

_____

_____

_____

_____

_____

_____

_____

_____

_____

_____

Devotion 25

As Job continued speaking to God, he painted a very dramatic word picture:

Job 13:27 *Thou puttest my feet also in the stocks, and lookest narrowly unto all my paths; thou settest a print upon the heels of my feet.* **28** *And he, as a rotten thing, consumeth, as a garment that is moth eaten.*

In verse twenty-seven, Job used the picture of a slave with stocks around his feet to keep him from ever running away. A man could walk in them, barely, but he could never run. And, worn for a long period of time, they left a mark on the heels that would never go away.

In verse twenty-eight, Job began to speak of himself in the third person. Pastor Wagner hates it when people do that...

Anyway, he pictured himself as a worn-out, rotten, moth-eaten piece of clothing. Taken together, those verses paint the picture of a man who believes that he is already as good as dead while still living, a man who has no more usefulness left in life.

And yet, by the end of the book, he was hearing the words "honey" from his wife, "dadda" from his kids, and even "paw paw," "great grandpa," and "great great grandpappy!" The man who thought he had outlived his usefulness had 130 more years of diaper and babysitting duty waiting for him!

DO be careful about assuming your useful days are done; there may come a day when you are so "useful" again that you actually wish they were!

Personal Notes:

_____

_____

_____

_____

_____

_____

_____

_____

_____

_____

_____

_____

_____

_____

_____

_____

_____

_____

_____

_____

_____

_____

_____

_____

_____

_____

_____

Devotion 26

We now come to one of the most famous verses in Job and the context that surrounds it.

Job 14:1 *Man that is born of a woman is of few days, and full of trouble.* **2** *He cometh forth like a flower, and is cut down: he fleeth also as a shadow, and continueth not.* **3** *And dost thou open thine eyes upon such an one, and bringest me into judgment with thee?* **4** *Who can bring a clean thing out of an unclean? not one.* **5** *Seeing his days are determined, the number of his months are with thee, thou hast appointed his bounds that he cannot pass;*

Man that is born of woman is of few days, and full of trouble. Job definitely got that one right, and James later wrote pretty extensively about that truth, even using Job's word picture about the flower in verse two.

But it is in verse five that we come to a pretty important truth of Scripture, especially since it clarifies something that people often get wrong. Using Hebrews 9:27, people often say, "The day of your death is an appointed thing. You aren't going to live one day less or one day more than God wants."

But that view is fifty percent wrong. Yes, we do have an appointment with death, and yes, God does know exactly when it will be. But Job correctly observed that "*thou hast appointed his bounds that he cannot pass.*" In other words, there is a certain number of days that we can never go beyond, no matter what. But whether or not we actually reach that number of days is not predetermined at all! Hundreds of times, the Bible gives commands with a "long life blessing" attached to them if we obey. And hundreds of times, the Bible also mentions people being cut off due to their sin.

Before you were ever born, God set a "maximum of days" for you, but not a minimum of days. So DO live your life in such a way that when you get to heaven, people there do not look at you and say, "Wait, you're here already? We weren't expecting you for another thirty years. What did you do, doofus?"

Personal Notes:

_____

_____

_____

_____

_____

_____

_____

_____

_____

_____

_____

_____

_____

_____

_____

_____

_____

_____

_____

_____

Devotion 27

Always remember that there are inaccuracies and errors in the Bible. Not in the text, mind you, but in what people said and thought within the text! The Bible accurately records for us things that people got right and things that people got wrong, truths that they told, and lies that they told as well. That will be important to remember as we get into the next several verses, where Job says things that are more cultish than Biblical!

Job 14:7 *For there is hope of a tree, if it be cut down, that it will sprout again, and that the tender branch thereof will not cease.* **8** *Though the root thereof wax old in the earth, and the stock thereof die in the ground;* **9** *Yet through the scent of water it will bud, and bring forth boughs like a plant.* **10** *But man dieth, and wasteth away: yea, man giveth up the ghost, and where is he?* **11** *As the waters fail from the sea, and the flood decayeth and drieth up:* **12** *So man lieth down, and riseth not: till the heavens be no more, they shall not awake, nor be raised out of their sleep.*

Picture going into Hobby Lobby and finding a plaque that says, "When You're Dead, You're Done!" I am guessing that would not be a good seller...

This is the same Job who in **Job 19:25-26** says, *"For I know that my redeemer liveth, and that he shall stand at the latter day upon the earth: And though after my skin worms destroy this body, yet in my flesh shall I see God."*

This is an excellent reminder that when reading Scripture, we need to be discerning about whether someone was speaking right words, or whether we are simply reading the inspired, preserved account of someone who was absolutely blowing it!

DO remember that it is the words of Scripture that are inspired, not necessarily everything that people like Job, Lucifer, Ananias and Saphira, Jezebel, and Peter had to say!

Personal Notes:

_____

_____

_____

_____

_____

_____

_____

_____

_____

_____

_____

_____

_____

_____

_____

_____

_____

_____

_____

_____

_____

_____

_____

_____

Devotion 28

Job continued to wax more and more despondent in his answer, to the point where he honestly started to sound a lot like Eeyore from Winnie the Pooh.

Job 14:17 *My transgression is sealed up in a bag, and thou sewest up mine iniquity.* **18** *And surely the mountain falling cometh to nought, and the rock is removed out of his place.* **19** *The waters wear the stones: thou washest away the things which grow out of the dust of the earth; and thou destroyest the hope of man.* **20** *Thou prevailest for ever against him, and he passeth: thou changest his countenance, and sendest him away.* **21** *His sons come to honour, and he knoweth it not; and they are brought low, but he perceiveth it not of them.* **22** *But his flesh upon him shall have pain, and his soul within him shall mourn.*

Ahem. "If it could ever be a good morning, which I doubt, I'd say that things will never change, but no one would listen to me anyway."

It really was that bad in his eyes. Job saw nothing but time eroding all things, and in the midst of all that, God just shoving one generation after another off to the side. That is really, really bleak!

But what is so instructive about it is that Job had no idea that we would be talking about it because he had no idea that someone was going to write it all down! So Job had 130 pleasant years for future generations to say, "Whoah, grandpop, you had a serious case of the mullygrubs!"

Before you whine, DO ask yourself, "Do I really want people to be showing me my Eeyore moments for the rest of my life?"

Personal Notes:

_____
_____
_____
_____
_____
_____
_____
_____
_____
_____
_____
_____
_____
_____
_____
_____
_____
_____
_____
_____
_____
_____
_____
_____
_____
_____
_____

Devotion 29

Eliphaz, who had already "had his say," now decides to rip into Job again. And while verses one through five are mostly just repetition of points that he had already made, we really do begin to get something new in verses six through ten that gives us very pertinent information and also insight into the thought process of Job's attackers.

Job 15:6 *Thine own mouth condemneth thee, and not I: yea, thine own lips testify against thee.* **7** *Art thou the first man that was born? or wast thou made before the hills?* **8** *Hast thou heard the secret of God? and dost thou restrain wisdom to thyself?* **9** *What knowest thou, that we know not? what understandest thou, which is not in us?* **10** *With us are both the grayheaded and very aged men, much elder than thy father.*

And there it is. Why were Job's three friends so pushy about getting him to agree that they were right and he was wrong? Why, because they were way older than him, and older people always have to be acknowledged as right by younger people! Or so a great many arrogant grayheads would have you believe.

Way back in my late twenties, I was at a function with a great many preachers. The old preacher in charge of it asked a question of all of us. I answered respectfully but honestly – even though I knew he was expecting everyone to simply "toe the company line." Through a very forced smile, he thanked me for what I said. And then the next day, he called me, screaming like a banshee over me "rebuking an elder in public," and making it very clear that since he was older, he was right. When he finally took a breath, I said, "Number one, you asked. Don't ever ask me a question if you don't want an honest answer. Number two, if you like, I will come to your place this very afternoon with a preacher who is older than you, who agrees with me. That way, you will have to agree that I am right since he is older than you, and therefore he is right. That is the way it works, according to you, isn't it?"

DO remind yourself that old people are due a measure of respect, but they are NOT due the assurance that they are right just because they manage to live long enough to be old!

Personal Notes:

_____

_____

_____

_____

_____

_____

_____

_____

_____

_____

_____

_____

_____

_____

_____

_____

_____

_____

Devotion 30

Continuing on in his second attack, Eliphaz utters some of the most infuriating words imaginable.

Job 15:11 *Are the consolations of God small with thee? is there any secret thing with thee? 12 Why doth thine heart carry thee away? and what do thy eyes wink at,* **13** *That thou turnest thy spirit against God, and lettest such words go out of thy mouth?*

When Eliphaz spoke of "the consolations of God," he was talking about the words that he and his two cohorts had been beating Job over the head with. In his view, Job thought he possessed secret knowledge, but he was really just too stupid to understand the wonderful gift God had sent him when He sent these three antagonists to him. Eliphaz believed that Job's heart was carried away with and his eyes winking at wickedness, and that is why he was speaking such ridiculous words.

Have you ever heard the phrase "God's gift to man?" With Eliphaz, this was not just a figure of speech; he literally believed that he and his friends and the bile they had been spewing were God's gift to Job!

People like that are such an incomprehensible joy to be around.

Before you ever decide to take that view of yourself, go take a good long look in the mirror. You will note that you are not covered in wrapping paper and do not have a shiny bow on the top of your head. DO have enough humility to view yourself as a simple servant of God rather than as the gift of God to mankind!

Personal Notes:

_____
_____
_____
_____
_____
_____
_____
_____
_____
_____
_____
_____
_____
_____
_____
_____
_____
_____
_____
_____
_____
_____
_____
_____
_____
_____
_____

Devotion 31

Eliphaz continued unabated in his second assault on Job. And in so doing, he did a marvelous job of whacking himself in the back of the head with a boomerang and not even realizing it.

Job 15:14 *What is man, that he should be clean? and he which is born of a woman, that he should be righteous?* **15** *Behold, he putteth no trust in his saints; yea, the heavens are not clean in his sight.* **16** *How much more abominable and filthy is man, which drinketh iniquity like water?* **17** *I will shew thee, hear me; and that which I have seen I will declare;*

In the view of Eliphaz, Job was declaring himself righteous when he should have been acknowledging his wickedness. And his reasoning, as seen in verses fifteen through sixteen, was that neither saints nor even the heavens themselves are clean in the sight of God; therefore, man is assuredly dirty in his sight. And while this is certainly true in a positional sense, it is by no means always true in a practical sense since even God Himself had declared Job to be a perfect and upright man. But the bigger issue to see, at this point, is that Eliphaz made that blanket statement about mankind and then turned right around and uttered the words, "*I will shew thee, hear me; and that which I have seen I will declare.*"

Do you see the problem? "All of mankind is horribly wicked and dirty, Job, so sit back and listen to me, a member of mankind, while I teach you the right way."

Houston, we have a problem.

Eliphaz said, "All of mankind is dirty," but what he really meant was, "Almost all of mankind is dirty; I'm actually pretty good myself." And isn't that the way people tend to view things? Throughout all of this, Job's three friends smeared him with one accusation of sin after another, but not a single one of them ever said, "Here is what I have done wrong." When we cannot even acknowledge our own sins and shortcomings, we should not be surprised that people do not want to hear us opine on theirs.

DO apply theological truth equally to everyone, including yourself!

Personal Notes:

_____

_____

_____

_____

_____

_____

_____

_____

_____

_____

_____

_____

_____

_____

_____

_____

_____

_____

Devotion 32

Eliphaz is now going to pull the "old guy card" again.

Job 15:18 *Which wise men have told from their fathers, and have not hid it:* **19** *Unto whom alone the earth was given, and no stranger passed among them.* **20** *The wicked man travaileth with pain all his days, and the number of years is hidden to the oppressor.*

From verse twenty-one through the end of the chapter, Eliphaz continues along this exact same line of thinking. It is, as before, his position that bad things ONLY happen to wicked people and ALWAYS happen to wicked people. And as proof, he tells Job to think back to the time of their fathers, when the earth was given, and no stranger passed among them. In other words, he was literally telling Job to think back to the time of Adam and Eve and their family.

And as you read that, you are doubtless already poking holes in Eliphaz's faulty theology. A sixth grader in Sunday school could do so. You see, Eliphaz was clearly focused on a man named Cain – without giving any thought whatsoever to a man named Abel. But Cain, while he spent his life under the judgment of God, also got married and had children and built cities and lived a long life. Abel, though, did everything right and, yet, never got to see old age. So, based just on exterior circumstances, things went far better for the one who lived wickedly than they did for the one who lived righteously.

It is both dangerous and incredibly frustrating to try and determine whether people are right with God or wrong with God based on the exterior circumstances of their lives. And yet that was the entirety of the basis for everything that the Musketeers of Misery said to Job. When we get like that, we will hurt others and sow doubts in our own hearts and homes. The wisest thing we can do is trust that, as Abraham said, "The judge of all the earth will surely do right," and then leave it up to Him to actually be the judge, rather than trying to nudge Him out of that seat based on the tiny little bit of sight and knowledge we have.

DO let the Judge be the judge!

Personal Notes:

_____

_____

_____

_____

_____

_____

_____

_____

_____

_____

_____

_____

_____

_____

_____

_____

_____

_____

_____

_____

Devotion 33

As Job 16 begins, Job will now begin to answer Eliphaz's second attack. As he does, you can almost hear the raw emotion in his voice.

Job 16:1 *Then Job answered and said,* **2** *I have heard many such things: miserable comforters are ye all.* **3** *Shall vain words have an end? or what emboldeneth thee that thou answerest?* **4** *I also could speak as ye do: if your soul were in my soul's stead, I could heap up words against you, and shake mine head at you.* **5** *But I would strengthen you with my mouth, and the moving of my lips should asswage your grief.*

"*Miserable comforters are ye all...*" Ouch. But accurate. From the time they began to open their mouths in chapter four, they have had little, if anything, actually comforting to say. And Job was correct to observe that if the tables were turned, he could just as easily say all of the things against them that they were saying against him. They hurled specific, filthy, unjust accusations against him for which they had no proof, so, since proof was apparently not needed, he certainly could do the exact same things to them if the situation were reversed.

But it was Job's assertion that, if the tables were turned, he would instead choose to say encouraging, helpful, comforting things to them to help assuage their grief. And that begs a question for us; would he? If they had been devastated and he had gone to them, would he have spoken comforting words to them, or would he have taken the same proud, haughty, caustic approach to them that they were taking with him? And the obvious answer is, we have no idea. Job had spent months suffering by this point, so he was a radically changed man than he was before.

We, therefore, do not know if Job would have comforted them in their time of trial previously; it is safe to say, though, that he would have comforted them in any trials after his own trials. Job now knew what it was like to be broken and hurting and thoroughly confused. Someone like that makes a great comforter for others going through the same thing.

Those horrible things that you have gone through or are going through? DO let them turn you into a compassionate person instead of a caustic person!

Personal Notes:

_____

_____

_____

_____

_____

_____

_____

_____

_____

_____

_____

_____

_____

_____

_____

_____

_____

_____

Devotion 34

We get a bit of a view of Job's heartaches and even his expectations when we compare verses five and six.

Job 16:5 *But I would strengthen you with my mouth, and the moving of my lips should asswage your grief.* **6** *Though I speak, my grief is not asswaged: and though I forbear, what am I eased?*

Viewing this through the lens of the parallelism of Hebrew poetry, we see that assuage in verse five matches up with assuaged in verse six, and strengthen in verse five matches up with eased in verse six. In other words, Job, having just told his attackers that, if the situation were reversed, he would comfort them, now points out how little comfort he is able to give himself. Had they spoken rightly, they could have strengthened him; but his speaking did not ease his pain a bit. Had they spoken rightly, they could have assuaged his grief. But nothing that he said assuaged his own grief in the least.

Think of it this way; it is hard to rescue a drowning person if you yourself are that drowning person.

Expecting a person just to "pick himself up by his bootstraps" is often a pretty ridiculous thing. There are times when, if we are going to get any comfort, it will have to come from others because there is nothing inside of us to comfort ourselves. So God allows us to sometimes be comforted by others and at other times to be the comforter of others. In so doing, He builds bonds between us that make us closer than ever before.

When you need comfort, DO be willing to receive it, and when others need comfort, DO be willing to give it!

Personal Notes:

_____

_____

_____

_____

_____

_____

_____

_____

_____

_____

_____

_____

_____

_____

_____

_____

_____

_____

_____

_____

_____

_____

_____

_____

Devotion 35

As he does so often throughout this book, Job will now once again segue from answering one of his attackers, Eliphaz, to speaking to God directly. And when he does, we learn a bit more about Job and about the things he was going through.

Job 16:7 *But now he hath made me weary: thou hast made desolate all my company. 8 And thou hast filled me with wrinkles, which is a witness against me: and my leanness rising up in me beareth witness to my face.*

Notice the shift from "he" to "thou" in verse seven. Job starts the verse by speaking about God to Eliphaz and ends the verse by speaking to God. He complains that God has *made desolate all his company."* And his company, meaning his companionship, was indeed desolate at that point. This man, who had only recently had a wife and ten children and servants and friends, has now found himself estranged from his wife, mourning the loss of all ten of his children, having servants who refused to attend to his needs (Job 19:16), and "friends" who are only attacking him.

But in verse eight, Job also begins to paint a verbal portrait of his face for us. His face is now wrinkled and lean. And the fact that this is a new thing for Job tells us that he was by no means an old man. But though he was not old, he now looked as if he had aged decades beyond his years. If you have ever seen one of those unfortunate people in their 40s or 50s who looks like they need to be in a nursing home somewhere, you are getting the idea. And while that may not seem like that big of a deal, all things considered, it was just another straw to break the camel's back for Job.

Sometimes we take note of all of the horrible things people are going through without even stopping to consider that they may also have a thousand tiny things weighing on them at the same time. So DO be sensitive to the Holy Spirit; sometimes handing someone a bit of lotion is every bit as comforting to them as telling them, "I will be praying for you!"

Personal Notes:

_____

_____

_____

_____

_____

_____

_____

_____

_____

_____

_____

_____

_____

_____

_____

_____

_____

_____

Devotion 36

As Job continues to speak to God, he moves from the subject of his face to the subject of his foes.

Job 16:9 *He teareth me in his wrath, who hateth me: he gnasheth upon me with his teeth; mine enemy sharpeneth his eyes upon me. 10 They have gaped upon me with their mouth; they have smitten me upon the cheek reproachfully; they have gathered themselves together against me. 11 God hath delivered me to the ungodly, and turned me over into the hands of the wicked.*

A question automatically arises from these verses: who was Job referring to when he described his enemies in this fashion? The terminology he uses is pretty brutal; "teareth me in his wrath, hateth me: gnasheth upon me with his teeth; sharpeneth his eyes upon me, gaped upon me with their mouth; smitten me upon the cheek reproachfully, gathered themselves together against me."

Commentators are pretty evenly divided on this. Everyone knows it is not God being spoken of since verse eleven says, *"God hath delivered me to the ungodly, and turned me over into the hands of the wicked."*

Some regard these adversaries of whom Job speaks as his three attacking friends. Others regard it as the devil and his demons who actually did all of the damage to Job. But from one point of view, it is utterly irrelevant which of those two things is correct. By that, I mean, if we even have to wonder whether or not it applies to these three men instead of devils and demons, then those three men really blew it! Anytime we behave ourselves in such a way that our words and our actions make people wonder if it is the

76

devil speaking and acting, we have really messed up royally.

DO make sure that if people mistake you for anyone, they mistake you for an angel rather than for a devil!

Personal Notes:

_____

_____

_____

_____

_____

_____

_____

_____

_____

_____

_____

_____

_____

_____

_____

_____

_____

_____

_____

_____

_____

_____

_____

_____

Devotion 37

Job went from speaking of his face to speaking of his foes and will now return to the subject of his physical appearance. And as before, it paints a bleak picture.

Job 16:15 *I have sewed sackcloth upon my skin, and defiled my horn in the dust.* **16** *My face is foul with weeping, and on my eyelids is the shadow of death;*

We find something utterly unique in verse fifteen. Job sewed sackcloth onto his body. That is not said anywhere else in Scripture. In every single one of the other forty-six references to sackcloth, people are said to have put it on, or to be laying in it, or something of that nature. But Job was so broken that he did not simply slip sackcloth over his body, he sewed it onto his body where it would not come off unless it were cut off.

Job also said that he had "defiled his horn in the dust." Horns were worn on headgear of important people to denote their authority. Job had taken his "captain's hat," if you will, and completely ruined it in the dirt, figuring to never wear it again.

His face was fouled with weeping; it had taken on the worn and puffy look of someone who has cried for a long time. His eyelids were black, as often happens to those who are sick for a very long time. Job looked really bad, and the fact that he sewed sackcloth on his body tells us that he never expected things to get any better. But do you realize what that means? There came a day when Job had to cut the sackcloth off!

Wearing sackcloth emotionally is one thing; sewing it on to you is quite another. DO keep your sackcloth loose so that it can be easily removed when God begins to turn the tide in your life!

Personal Notes:

_____

_____

_____

_____

_____

_____

_____

_____

_____

_____

_____

_____

_____

_____

_____

_____

_____

_____

_____

_____

_____

_____

_____

_____

_____

_____

_____

Devotion 38

Job will now once again assert his innocence and also make a very important plea that we need to examine.

Job 16:17 *Not for any injustice in mine hands: also my prayer is pure.* **18** *O earth, cover not thou my blood, and let my cry have no place.* **19** *Also now, behold, my witness is in heaven, and my record is on high.* **20** *My friends scorn me: but mine eye poureth out tears unto God.* **21** *O that one might plead for a man with God, as a man pleadeth for his neighbour!*

When Job asked the earth not to cover his blood, it was an allusion to the murder of Abel. He was asking the earth not to cover up the fact that he had been destroyed unjustly. But then he turned his attention to heaven and said, "*behold, my witness is in heaven, and my record is on high.*" Job was still confident in his innocence.

But it is in verse twenty-one that we find Job lamenting, "*O that one might plead for a man with God, as a man pleadeth for his neighbour!*" Job was thinking of the fact that when two neighbors are at odds one with the other, another person can go to the stronger of the two neighbors and plead the cause for the weaker of the two. Job wished that a man could do that for another man before God.

Ahem. **Job 42:7** *And it was so, that after the LORD had spoken these words unto Job, the LORD said to Eliphaz the Temanite, My wrath kindled against thee, and against thy two friends: for ye have not spoken of me the thing that is right, as my servant Job hath.* **8** *Therefore take unto you now seven bullocks and seven rams, and go to my servant Job, and offer up for yourselves a burnt offering; and*

*my servant Job shall pray for you: for him will I
accept: lest I deal with you after your folly, in that ye
have not spoken of me the thing which is right, like my
servant Job.*

Well, looky there.

DO pray for one another, because God DOES
listen!

Personal Notes:

_____

_____

_____

_____

_____

_____

_____

_____

_____

_____

_____

_____

_____

_____

_____

_____

_____

_____

_____

_____

_____

Devotion 39

The first few verses of chapter seventeen will be a whirlwind of Job switching back and forth between speaking to God and speaking to his adversaries.

Job 17:1 *My breath is corrupt, my days are extinct, the graves are ready for me.* **2** *Are there not mockers with me? and doth not mine eye continue in their provocation?* **3** *Lay down now, put me in a surety with thee; who is he that will strike hands with me?* **4** *For thou hast hid their heart from understanding: therefore shalt thou not exalt them.*

Job speaks to whoever will listen in verse one, commenting on his breath that is fouled by long-term sickness, and on the fact that the graves (the cemetery) was ready for him. Then in verse two he speaks to God about the fact that his three mocking tormentors are still there provoking him. But it is in verse three that things get pretty interesting. When Job said, "lay down now," he was not talking about them stretching out on the couch. It is a financial/gambling term as in, "put your bet down on the table." At the end of the verse, "Who is he that will strike hands with me" means "who wants to bet me?"

Job was tired of hearing their baseless claims; as far as he was concerned, it was time for them to "put their money where their mouth was."

In verse four, Job addresses God and says, in so many words, "they are saying such dumb things right now because you have taken away their ability to think smart thoughts. That is the only good explanation for the stupidity pouring out of their mouths."

What is really interesting is the fact that not a single one of them took Job up on his bet. They all claimed to believe in the all powerful God, so all of them knew it would not have been difficult for God to "speak up and settle their bet." But none of them, not a single one was willing to put up or shut up.

DO make your words more than just words; if you are not willing to back them up in some significant way, it is usually better not to say them to begin with!

Personal Notes:

_____

_____

_____

_____

_____

_____

_____

_____

_____

_____

_____

_____

_____

_____

_____

_____

_____

_____

Devotion 40

We will consider just one verse in this section of Job's complaint since it is of such a practical yet difficult nature.

Job 17:5 *He that speaketh flattery to his friends, even the eyes of his children shall fail.*

In these few words, Job was rightly inferring two things. One, his "friends" who had been attacking him for so long now wanted exactly one thing; they wanted Job to finally agree with them. Two, in order for Job to agree with them, he would have to flatter them since he could not do so truthfully.

Now, from Job's perspective, agreeing with the wrong words of his friends, flattering them as they desired, would actually have some immediate, short-term benefit. Had Job simply agreed to all of their charges and thanked them for being so kind as to point out all of his "wickedness," the attacks would have stopped, and they would have soothed their "properly chastised friend" with their words. All he had to do to make the pain they were delivering immediately stop was just agree with them...

But he would not do it. In his words, whoever does that kind of thing finds that "the eyes of his children shall fail." Yes, we know that Job's children were all already dead. But this was a euphemistic way of saying, "Others that come behind me will see me lying and flattering you for my benefit, and it will damage them."

Job was right in that. If we are ever perceived as people who flatter others to make things go easier for us, we will have either no influence or a negative influence on those who look up to us.

DO think enough of others to keep phony flattery from ever falling off of your lips!

Personal Notes:

_____

_____

_____

_____

_____

_____

_____

_____

_____

_____

_____

_____

_____

_____

_____

_____

_____

_____

_____

_____

_____

_____

_____

_____

_____

_____

_____

_____

Devotion 41

As Job continues his complaint, he uses a picturesque bit of Hebrew poetry to describe how conditions have changed for him.

Job 17:6 *He hath made me also a byword of the people; and aforetime I was as a tabret.*

The two words compared and contrasted in this verse are byword and tabret. Job says that he, most likely meaning God, has made Job a byword when before all of this started, he was a tabret. A byword means a taunt, a bit of mockery. In other words, Job was now the butt of everyone's jokes and insults. Before that, though, he had been like a pleasant musical instrument that everyone wanted to listen to.

That is an incredibly stark contrast. Job went from a tabret to a taunt, from a jewel to a joke. And when a person falls from public favor like that through immorality, they have no need to complain. Many a preacher, or even just an outspoken Christian, has so sullied their own reputation that they justly deserve whatever scorn is heaped upon them. But in Job's case, his behavior and morality had not changed in the least. His destruction was entirely from external circumstances, not from any internal failing. And yet the people that we can usually draw the most wisdom from are those who have suffered, not from those whose lives have been a fairy tale of ease and comfort. Thousands of years later, James did not have anything to say about Solomon, but he did mention the patience of Job!

DO be careful never to make your "tabret or taunt" evaluation of someone based on their external circumstances; Job had his legendary trials, Stephen was stoned to death, Jesus had nowhere to lay His head and died on Calvary, and all of them are far better choices for your "tabrets" than any Hollywood star or social media influencer on the planet!

Personal Notes:

_____

_____

_____

_____

_____

_____

_____

_____

_____

_____

_____

_____

_____

_____

_____

_____

_____

_____

_____

_____

_____

_____

Devotion 42

Having lamented his change from tabret to taunt, Job will now once again assess his condition and push back against his accusers.

Job 17:7 *Mine eye also is dim by reason of sorrow, and all my members are as a shadow.* **8** *Upright men shall be astonied at this, and the innocent shall stir up himself against the hypocrite.* **9** *The righteous also shall hold on his way, and he that hath clean hands shall be stronger and stronger.* **10** *But as for you all, do ye return, and come now: for I cannot find one wise man among you.*

Through constant weeping, Job's eyesight had been greatly weakened. His members, meaning the various parts of his body, were as a shadow, or as we would put it in modern vernacular, "he was a shadow of his former self."

In verses eight and nine, though, Job turns again to how his friends/adversaries were treating him and says that men would be astonished at all of his afflictions, and that innocent men would "stir themselves up against the hypocrite, meaning against Job's accusers. The righteous, though, meaning Job, would get stronger and stronger. And he ended this thought by saying, "*But as for you all, do ye return, and come now: for I cannot find one wise man among you.*" Adam Clarke paraphrases this well: "Go again to school, get back to your own houses, and endeavour to acquire humility and knowledge; for there is not one wise man among you."

Ouch!

In all of this, though, I find a most unusual comfort. Job was continually asking to die, and yet every time he was attacked, it riled him up at least momentarily and made him determined to live and prove them all wrong. And isn't that usually the way it is when we ourselves get unjustly attacked?

When people attack you, rather than wither up and die, DO thank God for the motivation it provides you to keep on going!

Personal Notes:

_____

_____

_____

_____

_____

_____

_____

_____

_____

_____

_____

_____

_____

_____

_____

_____

_____

_____

_____

_____

_____

_____

_____

Devotion 43

Notice the strength and hope with which Job ended the last two verses:

Job 17:9 *The righteous also shall hold on his way, and he that hath clean hands shall be stronger and stronger.* **10** *But as for you all, do ye return, and come now: for I cannot find one wise man among you.*

And now notice the tone of the next six verses:

Job 17:11 *My days are past, my purposes are broken off, even the thoughts of my heart.* **12** *They change the night into day: the light is short because of darkness.* **13** *If I wait, the grave is mine house: I have made my bed in the darkness.* **14** *I have said to corruption, Thou art my father: to the worm, Thou art my mother, and my sister.* **15** *And where is now my hope? as for my hope, who shall see it?* **16** *They shall go down to the bars of the pit, when our rest together is in the dust.*

The cracking sound that a whip makes is caused by it moving one direction, and then so violently being yanked the other direction that the loop breaks the sound barrier. That is a pretty good metaphor for the whiplash-type swings in Job's emotions – and often in ours. Be honest; have you ever felt a surge of faith, a swell of optimism, and then seconds later been in the very depths of despair? And have you often felt guilty over that seeming lack of emotional control?

Consider this devotion as a permission slip to stop feeling guilty. Your emotions are not the issue; your response is the issue. You cannot always keep your emotions from swinging. If you could, you would be a better person than Job, Elijah, David, Peter, John the Baptist, and the Apostle Paul!

What you can do, is do right anyway. God is not scoring your "feelings;" He is scoring your choices. He did not say, "It is required in stewards that a man be found happy," He said, "It is required in stewards that a man be found faithful."

No matter where your emotions are at any point on this roller coaster called life, DO be faithful!

Personal Notes:

_____

_____

_____

_____

_____

_____

_____

_____

_____

_____

_____

_____

_____

_____

_____

_____

_____

_____

_____

_____

_____

Devotion 44

After Job paused his speaking, Bildad spoke for a second time. Look, then, at how similar his words are in both of his opening diatribes:

Job 8:2 *How long wilt thou speak these things? and how long shall the words of thy mouth be like a strong wind?*

Job 18:2 *How long will it be ere ye make an end of words? mark, and afterwards we will speak.*

Please allow me to couch my feelings on Bildad in the most spiritual terms I possibly can: I want to reach through time, yank the snotty twerp up by the robe, and body slam him. And then pray over him. (See? I told you it would be spiritual!)

Bildad's snarky comment here, in our modern terms, is, "You just keep on yapping, Job. But whenever you are finally done, let us know, and then we will talk." And then he pulls the "offended card:"

Job 18:3 *Wherefore are we counted as beasts, and reputed vile in your sight?*

"Hey, Job, I know we have growled at you and chewed your face off and clawed you to pieces and ripped out your heart, but why are you treating us like animals?"

Grrrrr. Bildad is a great example of abusers of all sorts, physical, emotional, even spiritual, who constantly hurt others and then play the victim when they are called on it. And your life will get infinitely better the day you stop catering to people of that sort.

DO take good instruction, even when it hurts. But DO also think enough of the God who made you to decline the role of anyone's physical/emotional/spiritual punching bag!

Personal Notes:

_____
_____
_____
_____
_____
_____
_____
_____
_____
_____
_____
_____
_____
_____
_____
_____
_____
_____
_____
_____
_____
_____
_____
_____
_____
_____
_____

Devotion 45

As Bildad continues his second assault on Job, he insults Job yet again before quickly swerving back into "how little God thinks of Job."

Job 18:4 *He teareth himself in his anger: shall the earth be forsaken for thee? and shall the rock be removed out of his place?*

That first phrase, "*He teareth himself in his anger,*" is addressed to his two friends and is about Job. He was turned to Eliphaz and Zophar and said, in our terms, "Job has gone so insane that he is foaming at the mouth and is ripping his own flesh with his fingernails." Then he quickly turns back to Job and says, "*shall the earth be forsaken for thee? and shall the rock be removed out of his place?*" That set of phrases is a figure of speech meaning, "Do you think God is going to stop taking care of His world to give special attention and care to you?"

I am intrigued by that bit about anger. Was it true that Job was furiously angry? Absolutely. But the two questions we should ask about that are "when" and "why." Job was not at all angry in chapter one, or chapter two, or three. Nor was he angry when his children died, his wealth was stolen, and his health was wrecked. Job did not show the tiniest amount of anger until three supposed friends accused him of stealing from widows and breaking the arms of orphans and being the cause of his own children's death!

In other words, these guys gave him his reason to be angry and then feigned shock over his anger.

That really makes me... angry.

In this world, not everyone goes well together. Sometimes, in fact, people mix about as well as oil and water. If someone habitually gets you angry enough to rip your face (or theirs!) off, you might want to ask yourself if you look good in orange because that is where the situation will eventually lead.

DO put some space between you and people who manufacture anger for you!

Personal Notes:

_____

_____

_____

_____

_____

_____

_____

_____

_____

_____

_____

_____

_____

_____

_____

_____

_____

_____

_____

_____

_____

_____

_____

Devotion 46

From **Job 18:5-21**, Bildad once again asserts the belief that only the wicked are judged, and the wicked are always judged in this life for all to see. Here is a sampling:

Verse five, "*the light of the wicked shall be put out.*" Verse eight, "*he is cast into a net by his own feet.*" Verse nine, "*the robber shall prevail against him.*" Verse eleven, "*Terrors shall make him afraid on every side.*" Verse twelve, "*destruction shall be ready at his side.*" Verse thirteen, "*the firstborn of death shall devour his strength.*" Verse fourteen is pretty dramatic, "*His confidence shall be rooted out of his tabernacle, and it shall bring him to the king of terrors.*" Verse fifteen, "*brimstone shall be scattered upon his habitation.*" Verse seventeen, "*His remembrance shall perish from the earth, and he shall have no name in the street.*" The last half of verse eighteen is pretty interesting, he shall be "*chased out of the world.*" Not sure exactly how he thought that one would work.

And then in verse nineteen he even reaches out for obscure relatives, becoming the first person in the Bible to use the word nephew: "*He shall neither have son nor nephew among his people, nor any remaining in his dwellings.*" Imagine any nephews of Job at that point giving the minion style "Whaaaatttt?" And then he closes in verse twenty-one with "*Surely such are the dwellings of the wicked, and this is the place of him that knoweth not God.*"

Bildad just called Job a sinner who did not know God. It's a shame the Bildad could not have gone to heaven at that point and straightened God out on that one, don't you think? Somehow, God was under the impression that Job was a "perfect and upright man who feared God and eschewed evil."

Bildad is a great example of, "If you can't be right, at least be consistent in your wrongness."

It is a great idea to never be like Bildad. And in order to keep that from happening, DO practice the following phrase very often: "I could be wrong!"

Personal Notes:

_____

_____

_____

_____

_____

_____

_____

_____

_____

_____

_____

_____

_____

_____

_____

_____

_____

_____

_____

_____

Devotion 47

As Job begins to answer Bildad for a second time, we should take note of a numerical issue.

Job 19:1 *Then Job answered and said,* **2** *How long will ye vex my soul, and break me in pieces with words?* **3** *These ten times have ye reproached me: ye are not ashamed that ye make yourselves strange to me.*

In every culture and language including our own, people use figures of speech. We often say, "if I told you once, I've told you a thousand times..." though we do not mean literally and exactly one thousand times. We simply mean "a bunch." That is what Job was doing in verse three when he said, "these ten times have ye reproached me." But the bigger issue than the exact number is Job's assertion at the end of verse three, "ye are not ashamed that ye make yourselves strange to me."

Adam Clarke gives a superb paraphrase of that, saying, "When I was in affluence and prosperity, ye were my intimates, and appeared to rejoice in my happiness; but now ye scarcely know me, or ye profess to consider me a wicked man because I am in adversity. Of this, you had no suspicion when I was in prosperity! Circumstances change men's minds."

That has not changed much through the millennia. We are often guilty of evaluating people based on their circumstances rather than on their observed character. When people are successful, at anything, we often overlook their character flaws. But when people are beleaguered, we often overlook their good character and see flaws that aren't even there!

DO be in the habit of looking past the circumstances, good or bad, and actually taking note of people's character, because sometimes good people have bad circumstances and bad people have good circumstances!

Personal Notes:

_____

_____

_____

_____

_____

_____

_____

_____

_____

_____

_____

_____

_____

_____

_____

_____

_____

_____

_____

_____

_____

_____

_____

_____

_____

_____

Devotion 48

As Job continues to answer Bildad, he gives us three very rich verses for which we should be grateful.

Job 19:4 *And be it indeed that I have erred, mine error remaineth with myself.* **5** *If indeed ye will magnify yourselves against me, and plead against me my reproach:* **6** *Know now that God hath overthrown me, and hath compassed me with his net.*

Verse four is a claim from Job that, if he has done some wrong that he does not know about, it has only affected him. They have claimed that he has broken the arms of orphans and stolen from widows and yet have produced no witnesses to that, for there were none to be had. In fact, they had not presented a scrap of evidence, or any witnesses, or any proof at all to any wrong in the life of Job!

In verses five and six, though, Job takes that reasoning a step farther and reminds them that if they are dead set on being his judge and jury, they should know that God Himself has already stepped in and judged Job, and harshly. Now, Job was wrong on this, as we have already seen; it was Satan that leveled Job, not God. But he was right in the fact that God does not need any "assistant paddle-swingers!" If we actually believe that God is spanking someone, we have two logical choices. One, believe that He is not God enough to do a good job, and therefore pile on and "help." Two, believe that He IS God enough to do a good job, and stay out of His way!

In your mind, please get a picture of a paddle hanging beside the throne of God in heaven. On it is written the very large word, "chastisement." But look closer... closer... and DO notice the fine print underneath that big word. It says, "God's personal property. Keep your grubby little hands off of it, or I will use it on you!"

Personal Notes:

_____

_____

_____

_____

_____

_____

_____

_____

_____

_____

_____

_____

_____

_____

_____

_____

_____

_____

_____

_____

_____

_____

_____

_____

_____

Devotion 49

As Job continues his complaint, he gives the fullest insight yet as to what was going on in and around his household as he suffered. And it is a pitiful picture.

Job 19:13 *He hath put my brethren far from me, and mine acquaintance are verily estranged from me.* **14** *My kinsfolk have failed, and my familiar friends have forgotten me.* **15** *They that dwell in mine house, and my maids, count me for a stranger: I am an alien in their sight.* **16** *I called my servant, and he gave me no answer; I intreated him with my mouth.* **17** *My breath is strange to my wife, though I intreated for the children's sake of mine own body.* **18** *Yea, young children despised me; I arose, and they spake against me.* **19** *All my inward friends abhorred me: and they whom I loved are turned against me.*

Job's brethren, meaning his close relatives, had withdrawn from him. His acquaintances, people he had met along the way, were estranged from him, and that word means "were utterly disgusted at." People who were living with him and employed by him regarded him as an alien and a stranger, a person who did not even belong there.

In verse sixteen, Job lamented that he called and even implored his own personal servant, and the man would not even acknowledge that Job had spoken. Young children, who formerly looked on Job with reverence and admiration, now despised him for no reason. When Job stood up, rather than give a customary bow of respect, they mocked him. All of Job's inward, meaning most intimate friends, now abhorred him; his "besties" became his "worsties."

And in general, everyone Job loved turned against him.

But most heartbreaking of all is what we find in verse seventeen, where Job said, "*My breath is strange to my wife, though I intreated for the children's sake of mine own body.*" As we saw in Job 17:1, we see here again that disease had so ravaged Job that even his breath was rancid. If anyone should have been able to love him anyway, surely it would be his wife. Job found out, though, that even though he reminded her of ten children they had brought into the world together, she would not even remain in his presence.

And no one could see any of that from the outside looking in.

DO be tender to people; you have no way of knowing all of the heartache they are going through!

Personal Notes:

_____

_____

_____

_____

_____

_____

_____

_____

_____

_____

_____

_____

_____

_____

Devotion 50

Job has pulled back the veil and let us see what was going on in his home, and it was heartbreaking. Now he will use some very picturesque language, figures of speech that we still use thousands of years later, and beg for pity from his friends.

Job 19:20 *My bone cleaveth to my skin and to my flesh, and I am escaped with the skin of my teeth.* **21** *Have pity upon me, have pity upon me, O ye my friends; for the hand of God hath touched me.* **22** *Why do ye persecute me as God, and are not satisfied with my flesh?*

We still say, "He is just skin and bones." We still say, "By the skin of my teeth." Both are an indication of nothingness. A person whose skin and bones are sticking together has no meat left on his body. The teeth have no skin. This was Job's way of saying, "I have escaped death so very barely that I have nothing left." And it is then that Job simply breaks down in front of his friends/enemies imploring, "*Have pity upon me, have pity upon me, O ye my friends.*" This is Job falling apart, begging for pity, since there was nothing else that anyone could possibly give that would fix his problems. Job then asks, "*Why do ye persecute me as God, and are not satisfied with my flesh?*" That last phrase means, "So, you think I have done wrong. Even if I had, can you not look at how broken and ruined I am and be satisfied? Is this not enough for whatever it is you imagine I have done?"

It shouldn't even have to be said, but that shouldn't have had to be said.

When people are devastated, especially people whom we have previously called friends, pity should not be something they have to beg for from us. In fact, look at how James described God's feelings toward Job: **James 5:11** *Behold, we count them happy which endure. Ye have heard of the patience of Job, and have seen the end of the Lord; that the Lord is very pitiful, and of tender mercy.*

How interesting! Job's three attackers refused to show him any pity and believed they were doing God's bidding by withholding that pity. And yet God Himself did show Job pity!

Be like God, not like Job's attackers; DO show pity!

Personal Notes:

_____

_____

_____

_____

_____

_____

_____

_____

_____

_____

_____

_____

_____

_____

_____

_____

_____

Devotion 51

There is a unique thing that we do not normally consider when looking at the life and trials of Job. When we are going through trials, we reach for a Bible and open it to Psalm 23 or Psalm 37 or John 14 or Philippians 4, or any number of other great passages for encouragement. But Job never did that a single time. And the reason he never did that is because not one single word of the Bible had even been written yet! Thinking of that, notice what Job said and how beautifully ironic it was:

Job 19:23 *Oh that my words were now written! oh that they were printed in a book!* **24** *That they were graven with an iron pen and lead in the rock for ever!*

Sitting there in front of his friends, right at the point of death and actually wishing he could go ahead and die, Job wished with all of his heart that his words were written in a book somewhere and would be available forever. His friends were not listening to him, so Job thought that maybe if his words were written in a book, someone somewhere at some time would read them and learn the truth about him.

And do you know how we know this? Because his words are written in a book!

Job did not know there would ever be such a thing as a Bible. Job did not know there would ever be a book of Job. Job did not know that for thousands of years people would be marveling at his faith and drawing strength for their own trials through reading about his! Job did not know that his heartache had any meaning or purpose. But God did. God already had a penman sitting nearby, ready to write everything down for our benefit.

DO look at your Bible and thank God for it; the man who needed it most never even had access to it, because it did not exist in his day!

Personal Notes:

_____

_____

_____

_____

_____

_____

_____

_____

_____

_____

_____

_____

_____

_____

_____

_____

_____

_____

_____

_____

_____

_____

_____

_____

Devotion 52

Job has just lamented that there is no book in which his words were written. And then, having foreshadowed the coming of Scripture, he gives us some of the most glorious words that coming Scripture would ever have:

Job 19:25 *For I know that my redeemer liveth, and that he shall stand at the latter day upon the earth:* **26** *And though after my skin worms destroy this body, yet in my flesh shall I see God:* **27** *Whom I shall see for myself, and mine eyes shall behold, and not another; though my reins be consumed within me.*

The doctrine contained in these few words is beyond stunning. With no Bible whatsoever, Job somehow had a grasp of theology that many seminary graduates never attain! Let me give you some of it, point by point. 1. He knew that God was a personal God, not the unconcerned God of the deist. He called him MY redeemer. 2. He knew that there was such a thing as redemption, meaning that God saves sinners. 3. He knew that God was still alive, meaning that He is eternal. 4. He knew that the world was going to come to an end, he referenced the latter day. 5. He knew that the God of heaven was coming to earth, which we see happening all the way in Revelation 19! 6. He knew that even after his body was consumed by worms, he would be given a brand new physical body in which he would see God.

Job said all of this, and every single bit of it was later confirmed by Scripture. He knew it before Scripture, we know it because of Scripture.

We know!

Do your days seem weary, and are things confusing? DO spend today focusing on what you KNOW is coming!

Personal Notes:

_____

_____

_____

_____

_____

_____

_____

_____

_____

_____

_____

_____

_____

_____

_____

_____

_____

_____

_____

_____

_____

_____

_____

Devotion 53

Having just given such a list of spectacular points of theology, Job now, at the end of chapter nineteen, returns to a more "down to earth" matter.

Job 19:28 *But ye should say, Why persecute we him, seeing the root of the matter is found in me?* **29** *Be ye afraid of the sword: for wrath bringeth the punishments of the sword, that ye may know there is a judgment.*

This is the second time in this chapter, along with verse twenty-two, that Job accuses his friends of persecuting him, and it was an accurate assessment. In this case, Job puts some needed words in their mouths. He tells them that they ought to be saying, "Why are we persecuting Job? The root of the matter (his trials) is in him." In other words, they should be recognizing that none of this is about them. This is all between Job and God.

But then he gives them a pretty sharp warning, saying, *"Be ye afraid of the sword: for wrath bringeth the punishments of the sword, that ye may know there is a judgment."* He was bluntly telling them that God regarded their attacks as wicked and was going to punish and judge them because of what they were doing.

No matter which view you take of who is right and who is wrong in all of their arguments, Job's assertion in this case is unassailable. God does indeed regard verbal persecution as vile in His sight. Remember how He handled Korah, Dathan, and Abiram when they spoke evil against Moses, and even how He handled Moses' own sister, Miriam, when she did the same! To God, the old adage "Sticks and stone may break my bones, but words will never hurt me" is ridiculous. By all means, speak truth when you must speak; but never think for a moment that God does not notice when you use your words to tear others down!

DO choose your words carefully; every word that needlessly injures a human being injures someone that God loved enough to die for!

Personal Notes:

_____

_____

_____

_____

_____

_____

_____

_____

_____

_____

_____

_____

_____

_____

_____

_____

_____

_____

_____

_____

_____

_____

_____

_____

Devotion 54

The last time we heard from Zophar, in chapter eleven, he was accusing Job of being a liar. Now, as he begins his second diatribe, he changes tactics from denigrating Job to elevating himself.

Job 20:1 *Then answered Zophar the Naamathite, and said, 2 Therefore do my thoughts cause me to answer, and for this I make haste. 3 I have heard the check of my reproach, and the spirit of my understanding causeth me to answer.*

Zophar said "therefore," meaning because of what you have just said, "*my thoughts cause me to answer, and for this I make haste. I have heard the check of my reproach, and the spirit of my understanding causeth me to answer.*"

In our modern vernacular, Zophar was saying, "You have said something, whatever it was, but I am so brilliant that I instinctively know that you are wrong, so I simply must speak back up very quickly." Ironically, a few years ago, a man attacked me online and used Zophar's exact words as justification! He had no idea who he was quoting or how much of a jerk Zophar was being. Even commentator Adam Clarke, normally a very dry writer, got really worked up over Zophar, saying, "It has already been observed that Zophar was the most inveterate of all Job's enemies, for we really must cease to call them friends. He sets no bounds to his invective, and outrages every rule of charity. A man of such a bitter spirit must have been, in general, very unhappy."

Bullseye.

When someone truly believes that they are the smartest person around and that they, therefore, have an obligation to quickly speak up and correct everyone else for everything, they are, to put it bluntly, as appealing as the southern end of a north-bound mule.

People will either enjoy seeing you come or enjoy seeing you go, and that will normally correspond closely to how much of a know-it-all, nag-it-all you choose to be.

Sometime today, take a look at a sock. Get the picture of it in your mind. And when you feel the urge to "fix everybody dumber than you," DO "put a sock in it!"

Personal Notes:

_____

_____

_____

_____

_____

_____

_____

_____

_____

_____

_____

_____

_____

_____

_____

_____

_____

_____

_____

Devotion 55

Zophar, having announced that he is "burdened with glorious purpose," will now drop all of that stinky purpose on Job yet again.

Job 20:4 *Knowest thou not this of old, since man was placed upon earth,* **5** *That the triumphing of the wicked is short, and the joy of the hypocrite but for a moment?* **6** *Though his excellency mount up to the heavens, and his head reach unto the clouds;* **7** *Yet he shall perish for ever like his own dung: they which have seen him shall say, Where is he?*

This second attack of Zophar is a pretty twisted one, being mixed with a set of generally true maxims and a completely untrue application. Just as Psalm 37 makes wonderfully clear, the wicked do only thrive for a short time and then are cut off. That truth is a very encouraging one that believers everywhere draw comfort from. But Zophar flips that truth on its head by applying it backwards. Instead of teaching that wicked people are cut off, he instead tries to infer that if people are cut off, they are wicked! And the Bible never, ever teaches that. In fact, **Isaiah 53:8**, speaking prophetically of Jesus Himself, says, "*He was taken from prison and from judgment: and who shall declare his generation? for he was cut off out of the land of the living: for the transgression of my people was he stricken.*"

In Zophar's mind, Job was the wicked hypocrite, not the innocent victim. To Zophar, there literally was no such thing as an innocent victim; if you suffer, you are sinful. It is very clear that Zophar was born with a silver spoon in his mouth, spoiled rotten, and perpetually pampered.

DO distinguish between cause and effect. The effect, in Job's case, was devastation in his life. But the cause was Satan, not sin!

Personal Notes:

_____

_____

_____

_____

_____

_____

_____

_____

_____

_____

_____

_____

_____

_____

_____

_____

_____

_____

_____

_____

_____

_____

_____

Devotion 56

Zophar, the most insulting of all of these miserable comforters, just keeps picking up steam as he railroads Job yet again. We often see all of these words in the book of Job and just skim over them as "argument number two of Zophar," but we should not because Job doubtless did not. Look at a few more verses of this vile invective, and let the meaning of them sink in.

Job 20:10 *His children shall seek to please the poor, and his hands shall restore their goods.* **11** *His bones are full of the sin of his youth, which shall lie down with him in the dust.* **12** *Though wickedness be sweet in his mouth, though he hide it under his tongue;* **13** *Though he spare it, and forsake it not; but keep it still within his mouth:* **14** *Yet his meat in his bowels is turned, it is the gall of asps within him.*

Zophar began by referencing the effects on the children of the wicked, knowing good and well that Job was staring at the ten graves of his own children, whose bodies were practically still warm. Then he taunted Job about "the sins of his youth" without ever bothering to offer details or proof. Then he slyly accused Job of having a filthy mouth and topped it all off by accusing Job of being as poisonous as a snake.

Let me remind you, he was there to "comfort" Job. To quote that legendary theologian, Inigo Montoya, "I do not think that word means what you think it means."

Even if Zophar was right (which he was not, at all), does this even seem like remotely good timing and setting? Is a graveyard, right after a man has buried ten children, and while he himself is at the brink of death, really the time and place to rip a man open and pour salt in every one of his wounds? And yet, while we have covered all of this time and again, another thought strikes me as I look at this: why did none of the other "friends" at any point say to him, "Hey, that's taking it a bit too far, and this really isn't the time."

It is easy to get so caught up in the fervor of "attacking them," whoever "them" is, that we fail to realize our responsibility to stand up and say, "You need to stop, that isn't appropriate."

DO be a real friend, one who is willing to call "your own side" on the carpet when necessary!

Personal Notes:

_____

_____

_____

_____

_____

_____

_____

_____

_____

_____

_____

_____

_____

_____

_____

_____

_____

_____

Devotion 57

Picking up steam like a runaway train, Zophar now gives several more descriptions of what is coming for Job and follows it up with another wild, unfounded accusation against him.

Job 20:15 *He hath swallowed down riches, and he shall vomit them up again: God shall cast them out of his belly.* **16** *He shall suck the poison of asps: the viper's tongue shall slay him.* **17** *He shall not see the rivers, the floods, the brooks of honey and butter.* **18** *That which he laboured for shall he restore, and shall not swallow it down: according to his substance shall the restitution be, and he shall not rejoice therein.* **19** *Because he hath oppressed and hath forsaken the poor; because he hath violently taken away an house which he builded not;*

According to Zophar, Job is going to puke up his wealth, drink snake venom, be bitten by a snake, not see pleasant things like water, honey, and butter, be forced to give away all he has worked for, and not be able to take satisfaction in any of his labor. And what, pray tell, would cause such a litany of punishment to fall on Job? Because Zophar was quite sure that Job had forsaken the poor and violently stolen someone else's house. He had kicked in the door, beaten everyone up, chased them out into the cold, and taken possession of their home.

But do you notice what Zophar does not give in all of that? He does not give any names, addresses, dates, witnesses, nothing. Just hideous accusations with no proof whatsoever. And poor Job, in his anguish of mind, body, and spirit, never did stop and say, "Okay, Jack, put up or shut up. Name names. Show the receipts."

One of the most cowardly things on earth is the unfounded accusation, especially the anonymous unfounded accusation. At least in Job's case, the one thing he did not have to deal with was social media! Can you imagine Zophar with a Facebook page and a Twitter account?

DO refrain from unfounded accusations, and DO be in the habit of demanding proof of anyone who makes them!

Personal Notes:

_____

_____

_____

_____

_____

_____

_____

_____

_____

_____

_____

_____

_____

_____

_____

_____

_____

_____

_____

_____

Devotion 58

Zophar will finish his second attack with a flourish. Let his words sink in as you read them.

Job 20:20 *Surely he shall not feel quietness in his belly, he shall not save of that which he desired.* **21** *There shall none of his meat be left; therefore shall no man look for his goods.* **22** *In the fulness of his sufficiency he shall be in straits: every hand of the wicked shall come upon him.* **23** *When he is about to fill his belly, God shall cast the fury of his wrath upon him, and shall rain it upon him while he is eating.* **24** *He shall flee from the iron weapon, and the bow of steel shall strike him through.* **25** *It is drawn, and cometh out of the body; yea, the glittering sword cometh out of his gall: terrors are upon him.* **26** *All darkness shall be hid in his secret places: a fire not blown shall consume him; it shall go ill with him that is left in his tabernacle.* **27** *The heaven shall reveal his iniquity; and the earth shall rise up against him.* **28** *The increase of his house shall depart, and his goods shall flow away in the day of his wrath.* **29** *This is the portion of a wicked man from God, and the heritage appointed unto him by God.*

All of these horrors that Zophar derisively tells Job are coming on him, he describes in verse twenty-nine as Job's "portion and heritage" from God. Portion means "your share," and heritage means "your inheritance." In other words, Zophar is picturing God as opening His last will and testament and saying, "Job, because you have been so rotten, here is what I am leaving you."

We know Zophar was insulting Job in this, but has it dawned on you that he was, though he could not see it, also insulting God? Zophar is picturing God as being hideously deficient. God, to him, was all anger and wrath and holiness and demands. God had no mercy, just hatred for the wicked and smug pride over the righteous. In fact, none of Job's three accusers ever even used the word "mercy!"

When you think on God today, DO think much on His mercy, because God is just as perfect at mercy as He is at judgment!

Personal Notes:

_____

_____

_____

_____

_____

_____

_____

_____

_____

_____

_____

_____

_____

_____

_____

_____

_____

_____

_____

_____

Devotion 59

Job will now begin to answer Zophar's second attack. But before he gets into the substance of his rebuttal, he spends a few verses giving a few "personal notes" about and to his friends.

Job 21:1 *But Job answered and said,* **2** *Hear diligently my speech, and let this be your consolations.* **3** *Suffer me that I may speak; and after that I have spoken, mock on.*

The Family Bible Notes gives a good paraphrase of verse two, saying, "If you will candidly listen to me, I will accept this in place of the consolations I might have so reasonably expected of you." Job just wanted his friends to actually listen to him; that would have been ample comfort. Sadly, though, he knew that was not going to happen, because he immediately followed that up by saying, "*Suffer me that I may speak; and after that I have spoken, mock on.*"

Isn't it a bit sad that Job wanted someone to listen but already knew that they were not going to do so and were instead going to mock him? These men were simply mean. They came to comfort a "friend," and when he did not agree with their assessment, they spent the rest of their time cutting him to ribbons.

A car will cost you a lot. A home will cost you a lot. Even groceries will cost you a lot these days. But kindness? That costs you nothing, and it means the world to whoever you give it to. So DO be kind today!

Personal Notes:

_____
_____
_____
_____
_____
_____
_____
_____
_____
_____
_____
_____
_____
_____
_____
_____
_____
_____
_____
_____
_____
_____
_____
_____
_____
_____
_____
_____

Devotion 60

As Job continued to answer Zophar a second time, look at the view that he gave of the wicked.

Job 21:7 *Wherefore do the wicked live, become old, yea, are mighty in power?* **8** *Their seed is established in their sight with them, and their offspring before their eyes.* **9** *Their houses are safe from fear, neither is the rod of God upon them.* **10** *Their bull gendereth, and faileth not; their cow calveth, and casteth not her calf.* **11** *They send forth their little ones like a flock, and their children dance.* **12** *They take the timbrel and harp, and rejoice at the sound of the organ.* **13** *They spend their days in wealth, and in a moment go down to the grave.*

Just moments earlier, Zophar had given his view of the wicked, and it was 180 degrees different! Job said the wicked grow old and become mighty in power (21:7), but Zophar said that the triumphing of the wicked is short, and the joy of the hypocrite but for a moment (20:5). Job said that their children are healthy and safe (21:8), but Zophar said the opposite in 20:10 and 20:28. Job said that their livestock would grow and be valuable (21:10), but Zophar said that "*his goods shall flow away in the day of his wrath.*" (28:10)

So which view was right? The answer is, "it depends on who you are watching." Sometimes things go exactly like Zophar said, and sometimes they go exactly as Job said! The mistake both of them made was assuming an "always" instead of observing the "sometimes." Assuming that God always deals with the wicked in the exact same way and on the exact same timetable is ludicrous and unbiblical! They will all end up the same, but in the meantime, their situations are often radically different.

If you want to avoid extreme frustration in life, DO refrain from assuming that God "must" do something and must do it a particular way and on a particular timetable!

Personal Notes:

_____

_____

_____

_____

_____

_____

_____

_____

_____

_____

_____

_____

_____

_____

_____

_____

_____

_____

_____

_____

_____

_____

_____

Devotion 61

As he continued speaking of the case of the wicked, even though he had made a wrong assumption about what God must "always" do, Job then made an absolutely correct assertion about the general thought process of the wicked.

Job 21:13 *They spend their days in wealth, and in a moment go down to the grave.* **14** *Therefore they say unto God, Depart from us; for we desire not the knowledge of thy ways.* **15** *What is the Almighty, that we should serve him? and what profit should we have, if we pray unto him?*

Notice those words "wealth" and "profit." Job is observing that when man is wicked yet highly successful, that very success keeps him from God. To the rich sinner, the bottom line is the bottom line. And since God is not "profitable" to his wallet, he reasons that he does not need God. You may remember that Jesus made the exact same observation many years later:

Mark 10:23 *And Jesus looked round about, and saith unto his disciples, How hardly shall they that have riches enter into the kingdom of God!* **24** *And the disciples were astonished at his words. But Jesus answereth again, and saith unto them, Children, how hard is it for them that trust in riches to enter into the kingdom of God!* **25** *It is easier for a camel to go through the eye of a needle, than for a rich man to enter into the kingdom of God.*

I often hear people lament the plight of the poor. But based on these passages, poverty may just be a gift from God in some cases! The God who wants everyone to be saved seems to keep some people poor, knowing that they will seek after Him in their poverty but would never do so in their wealth.

When you see the poor, do not assume that God is unkind to allow such situations. In fact, DO assume that it may be His very kindness that has allowed it!

Personal Notes:

_____

_____

_____

_____

_____

_____

_____

_____

_____

_____

_____

_____

_____

_____

_____

_____

_____

_____

_____

_____

Devotion 62

Job spent from verse sixteen through twenty-one telling Zophar that God often brings hard times down upon both the wicked and the righteous. This was a position that he bounced back to often, right in the midst of opining that the wicked always fared well. And this was obviously the more correct of his views.

After having done that, though, here is what he told Zophar next:

Job 21:22 *Shall any teach God knowledge? seeing he judgeth those that are high.* **23** *One dieth in his full strength, being wholly at ease and quiet.* **24** *His breasts are full of milk, and his bones are moistened with marrow.* **25** *And another dieth in the bitterness of his soul, and never eateth with pleasure.* **26** *They shall lie down alike in the dust, and the worms shall cover them.*

There was another mixture of accuracy and error in what Job said here. It was accurate to say that no one could teach God anything and that God judges those that are powerful and prominent. But the fatalism of verses twenty-four through twenty-six was certainly not accurate. Job was opining that everything we do, good or bad, is useless when it comes to our lot in life; God is just going to do what He wants to do, and then we all die.

Can you imagine ever convincing anyone to live right with that sales pitch? Thankfully, Galatians 6:7-8 teaches otherwise, as do many other verses. There is a reward to doing right, and much of that reward comes before the grave, not just after it.

DO right, because it DOES pay present dividends!

Personal Notes:

_____
_____
_____
_____
_____
_____
_____
_____
_____
_____
_____
_____
_____
_____
_____
_____
_____
_____
_____
_____
_____
_____
_____
_____
_____
_____
_____
_____
_____
_____
_____

Devotion 63

If you have ever tried to talk to someone and watched their faces as you did, you can understand what you see next as Job speaks.

Job 21:27 *Behold, I know your thoughts, and the devices which ye wrongfully imagine against me.* **28** *For ye say, Where is the house of the prince? and where are the dwelling places of the wicked?* **29** *Have ye not asked them that go by the way? and do ye not know their tokens,* **30** *That the wicked is reserved to the day of destruction? they shall be brought forth to the day of wrath.* **31** *Who shall declare his way to his face? and who shall repay him what he hath done?* **32** *Yet shall he be brought to the grave, and shall remain in the tomb.* **33** *The clods of the valley shall be sweet unto him, and every man shall draw after him, as there are innumerable before him.* **34** *How then comfort ye me in vain, seeing in your answers there remaineth falsehood?*

Job was clearly pretty heated in these words. When he said, "*Behold, I know your thoughts, and the devices which ye wrongfully imagine against me,*" he was basically saying, "I can see this written on your faces." He knew that having heard what he just said, they were going to ask him for any proof of the wicked faring well (v.28). Then he said, "Have ye not asked them that go by the way?"

He was telling them to talk to people that travel. In other words, "You guys clearly don't get around much, so why don't you ask anyone who does?" He then described again the oft-pleasant lives of the wicked, which worldwide travelers would see and observe. He closed his argument by saying, "*How then comfort ye me in vain, seeing in your answers there remaineth falsehood?"* In other words, "Your 'comfort' is hollow and empty because it still has lies all in it!"

Job gave good advice. Rather than evaluate everything by the handful of people we know, DO look farther afield; a wider view provides a better perspective!

Personal Notes:

_____

_____

_____

_____

_____

_____

_____

_____

_____

_____

_____

_____

_____

_____

_____

_____

_____

_____

_____

_____

Devotion 64

Eliphaz will now begin his third attack against Job. And right at the outset, he will say something mind-numbingly stupid.

Job 22:1 *Then Eliphaz the Temanite answered and said,* **2** *Can a man be profitable unto God, as he that is wise may be profitable unto himself?* **3a** *Is it any pleasure to the Almighty, that thou art righteous?*

Is it any pleasure to the Almighty, that thou art righteous...

Please bear with me for a moment as I transport myself back in time. Cue the Dr. Who sounds...

"Hello, Eliphaz, nice to meet you. You don't know me, and I know my clothes look a bit funny to you, but I wanted to bring you a message. You may not understand it, but here goes. You, sir, have an elevator that does not go all the way to the top, your driveway does not quite reach the road, you are a few fries short of a happy meal, your lights are on but no one is home, and your ladder is missing all of its top rungs. Thanks, I'll just hop back in my handy-dandy time machine and be moseying along, now..."

Yes, God is pleased by our righteousness. In order to believe that He is NOT pleased by our righteousness, we must believe that He commands us to be righteous and then is still as ill as a hornet at us even when we are. God is not like that, at all.

DO develop a better view of God than Eliphaz. He is the King of kings, not the King of Karens!

Personal Notes:

Devotion 65

Eliphaz is now going to rip into Job again with a series of brutal allegations.

Job 22:5 *Is not thy wickedness great? and thine iniquities infinite?* **6** *For thou hast taken a pledge from thy brother for nought, and stripped the naked of their clothing.* **7** *Thou hast not given water to the weary to drink, and thou hast withholden bread from the hungry.* **8** *But as for the mighty man, he had the earth; and the honourable man dwelt in it.* **9** *Thou hast sent widows away empty, and the arms of the fatherless have been broken.*

Eliphaz first makes a general claim that Job's sin is literally infinite. That is both stupid and impossible. But he then accuses him specifically of stealing the collateral of a brother who was in debt to him. Then he accuses Job of taking clothes from people to the point of making them naked. He accuses him of not giving water and bread to those in need. He accuses him of withholding help from poor widows. He lastly accuses him of breaking the arms of fatherless children!

And either God was lying when He called Job a perfect and upright man or Eliphaz was lying when he made these accusations. It is safe to say that Eliphaznocchio was the liar here...

But how many times have very good people been ruined by very good liars? We have the book of Job to read and discern the truth about Job, but not everybody gets a book. That being the case, the more sensational the accusation we hear, the more skeptical we should be and the more investigation we should do before ever repeating it.

DO refrain from helping an Eliphaz build an audience!

Personal Notes:

_____

_____

_____

_____

_____

_____

_____

_____

_____

_____

_____

_____

_____

_____

_____

_____

_____

_____

_____

_____

_____

_____

_____

Devotion 66

There is a really critical word in what Eliphaz says next, a word that often goes overlooked but definitely should not.

Job 22:10 *Therefore snares are round about thee, and sudden fear troubleth thee;* **11** *Or darkness, that thou canst not see; and abundance of waters cover thee.*

Therefore. That word is often simply skimmed over, but it is a really key word! It means "because of this." In other words, the horrible accusations Eliphaz made about Job in verses five through nine were, in his mind, the "therefore," the specific reason that Job had "snares" and "sudden fear" and "darkness" and "abundance of waters covering him," which is a figurative way of saying that he was drowning. But is that the "therefore" that God gave? Not at all! The therefore that God gave was that the devil showed up and had noticed both Job's righteousness and Job's blessings and was angry over both. That is a very different "therefore!"

Therefores are, to finite humans, usually a bit of a speculation game. If we see some redneck say, "Watch this, y'all!" then the "therefore" is usually pretty clear, as in, "Man, we're sure gonna miss Bubba, but that's what you get when you get drunk and try to kiss a rattlesnake!" But in most cases, things are nowhere near as clear. What does cancer or a fire or a tragic wreck have to do with anything most of the time? We humans are so prone to speculate, but that is usually all that it is, speculation.

DO be very careful of your "therefores," because you may be completely wrong about what the hardships in someone else's life are "there for!"

Personal Notes:

_____

_____

_____

_____

_____

_____

_____

_____

_____

_____

_____

_____

_____

_____

_____

_____

_____

_____

_____

_____

_____

_____

_____

_____

_____

_____

_____

Devotion 67

Eliphaz's next set of assertions is, once again, infuriating.

Job 22:12 *Is not God in the height of heaven? and behold the height of the stars, how high they are!* **13** *And thou sayest, How doth God know? can he judge through the dark cloud?* **14** *Thick clouds are a covering to him, that he seeth not; and he walketh in the circuit of heaven.*

Eliphaz acknowledged that God is above all and in the height of heaven. No problem, so far. But then he segued from that into saying that because of that, Job, said, *"How doth God know? can he judge through the dark cloud? Thick clouds are a covering to him, that he seeth not; and he walketh in the circuit of heaven."* In other words, "How does God know anything about us? He does not even see what is going on with us. If only God could see and know everything; if only He cared!"

There is just one teensy problem; Job literally never said any of that. Search the entire book of Job up to this point, it simply isn't there! Eliphaz put every word of that in Job's mouth and then proceeded to attack it. This is what is known as a straw man argument. The picture is of a person who has an enemy, but rather than actually face off against that enemy, they build a likeness of him out of straw and proceed to beat the stuffing out of it as if it was real.

Observing these verses, Adam Clarke said, "These were sentiments which Job never held, and never uttered; but if a man be dressed in a bear's skin, he may be hunted and worried by his own dogs. Job's friends attribute falsities to him, and then dilate upon them, and draw inferences from them injurious to his character. Polemic writers, both in theology and politics, often act in this way."

That is eloquent and accurate. But allow me, please, to put it in simpler terms. If you have to make a straw man to fight, the problem is not that the straw man has no brain, the problem is that you are a cowardly lion that has no courage!

DO deal with actual words and issues, not imaginary words and issues that you attribute to others!

Personal Notes:

_____

_____

_____

_____

_____

_____

_____

_____

_____

_____

_____

_____

_____

_____

_____

_____

_____

_____

_____

_____

Devotion 68

Barreling on down the insult tracks like a freight train being fueled by cow patties, Eliphaz delivers yet another pious-sounding lesson ending with another stab to Job's heart.

Job 22:15 *Hast thou marked the old way which wicked men have trodden?* **16** *Which were cut down out of time, whose foundation was overflown with a flood:* **17** *Which said unto God, Depart from us: and what can the Almighty do for them?* **18** *Yet he filled their houses with good things: but the counsel of the wicked is far from me.* **19** *The righteous see it, and are glad: and the innocent laugh them to scorn.* **20** *Whereas our substance is not cut down, but the remnant of them the fire consumeth.*

In verses fifteen and sixteen, Eliphaz gives Job the EXACT same argument he and his friends have been giving the entire time, that wicked people are always cut down and ruined by God in this life. It is as if Eliphaz is an old phonograph with only one record, and the needle is stuck. Then in verse seventeen, he pictures the wicked (including Job) as telling God to buzz off. In verse eighteen, he sarcastically uses Job's own words from 21:14 and 21:16 against him.

It is in verse twenty, though, that he really gets cutthroat with Job, saying, "*Whereas our substance is not cut down, but the remnant of them the fire consumeth.*" In other words, "Hey, Job, in case you can't figure out who the righteous people are around here, take a look at the bottom line. Your kids are dead; ours are alive. Your flocks are gone; ours are safe. Your wealth has vanished, and we are still loaded."

To Eliphaz, the greatest proof of a person's righteousness was their bank account. Which makes sense, right? I mean, politicians and porn stars and mafia bosses and drug lords are all in poverty...

No. They're not. And no, riches is not proof of righteousness.

DO separate riches and righteousness in your mind, because if riches are proof of righteousness, Christ Himself must have been the most unrighteous of all!

Personal Notes:

_____

_____

_____

_____

_____

_____

_____

_____

_____

_____

_____

_____

_____

_____

_____

_____

_____

Devotion 69

Still focused like a laser beam on the subject of riches, Eliphaz will now piously tell Job how to fix all of his problems.

Job 22:21 *Acquaint now thyself with him, and be at peace: thereby good shall come unto thee.* **22** *Receive, I pray thee, the law from his mouth, and lay up his words in thine heart.* **23** *If thou return to the Almighty, thou shalt be built up, thou shalt put away iniquity far from thy tabernacles.* **24** *Then shalt thou lay up gold as dust, and the gold of Ophir as the stones of the brooks.* **25** *Yea, the Almighty shall be thy defence, and thou shalt have plenty of silver.*

Acquaint thyself with God... These words were spoken to a man who had just lost everything BECAUSE of how well acquainted he was with God, and God was with him!

Then came "return to the Almighty." But when, pray tell, did Job ever "leave" the Almighty?

But Eliphaz was quite sure that he knew what he knew. And he informed Job that if he would just "come to know God," God would make him so rich that he would have gold like the dust and stones of the earth. Eliphaz and Company were very little different from the modern prosperity pimps of the Prosperity Gospel crowd. Their camels probably had "Bentley" engraved on their butts, and their tents likely had gold facades.

Nothing, absolutely nothing is as far from the truth of Scripture as the filthy, slimly, prosperity gospel. And if you "sow a seed of faith" in the ministry of any of them, you have an IQ number that would not make for a respectable earthquake.

DO have a healthy disdain for "name it and claim it" theology!

Personal Notes:

_____

_____

_____

_____

_____

_____

_____

_____

_____

_____

_____

_____

_____

_____

_____

_____

_____

_____

_____

_____

_____

_____

_____

Devotion 70

Eliphaz was wrapping up his latest sloppy screed, and in the midst of that wrap up, he uttered yet another mind-numbingly ridiculous assertion.

Job 22:26 *For then shalt thou have thy delight in the Almighty, and shalt lift up thy face unto God.* **27** *Thou shalt make thy prayer unto him, and he shall hear thee, and thou shalt pay thy vows.* **28** *Thou shalt also decree a thing, and it shall be established unto thee: and the light shall shine upon thy ways.* **29** *When men are cast down, then thou shalt say, There is lifting up; and he shall save the humble person.* **30** *He shall deliver the island of the innocent: and it is delivered by the pureness of thine hands.*

Right in the midst of those verses "encouraging Job to get right with God," Eliphaz said, *"Thou shalt also decree a thing, and it shall be established unto thee."* As with what we saw in the previous devotion, this is actually, literally, what the proponents of the prosperity gospel believe. They believe that if you say it as if it already is, God is obligated to make it come to be just like you have spoken it.

Pretty sure God never got the memo on that one.

I have a book in my library that teaches people to decree things just like this. Chapter five teaches you how to decree that your wife is perfect in every way. Chapter six teaches you to decree that your husband is perfect in every way. Cool, right?

Not so much; chapter seven teaches you how to pray over your troubled marriage! Why, pray tell, would anyone need to pray over a troubled marriage when their spouse is perfect?

It is not just illogical, it is unbiblical. God never gave you the power to decree anything. Decrees come from the King, not from His subjects.

DO know your place, and God's throne is not it!

Personal Notes:

_____

_____

_____

_____

_____

_____

_____

_____

_____

_____

_____

_____

_____

_____

_____

_____

_____

_____

_____

_____

_____

_____

_____

_____

_____

Devotion 71

Eliphaz was now finished his attacks, and Job was getting ready to speak at length, with one small interruption from Bildad. And as he began to speak again, he said something pretty interesting and instructive.

Job 23:1 *Then Job answered and said,* **2** *Even to day is my complaint bitter: my stroke is heavier than my groaning.*

My stroke is heavier than my groaning. By stroke, he meant the stroke of misfortune that had fallen upon him. He was saying, "Yes, I am complaining bitterly. But I am actually saying less than I could say, and complaining less than my situation warrants."

Now, that is a subjective statement. It is an opinion, and we have no way to measure or weigh it for accuracy. But it does teach us something pretty valuable, namely that between over complaining or under complaining, under complaining is normally the best option by far! When people over complain, not only are they showing a lack of gratitude, they are also ensuring that people will fail to take them seriously when things truly are bad! They also tend to push people away; who wants to be around someone that treats every headache as if it is the migraine to end all migraines, and every simple disagreement as if someone is out to destroy them?

DO lean more toward under-complaint than over-complaint!

Personal Notes:

_____

_____

_____

_____

_____

_____

_____

_____

_____

_____

_____

_____

_____

_____

_____

_____

_____

_____

_____

_____

_____

_____

_____

_____

_____

_____

_____

Devotion 72

Job will now utter some pretty shocking words, words that are, at once, words of great confidence and words of great error.

Job 23:3 *Oh that I knew where I might find him! that I might come even to his seat! 4 I would order my cause before him, and fill my mouth with arguments. 5 I would know the words which he would answer me, and understand what he would say unto me. 6 Will he plead against me with his great power? No; but he would put strength in me. 7 There the righteous might dispute with him; so should I be delivered for ever from my judge.*

Job wanted a chance to come before God's judgment seat and plead his case. He believed that he and God would have an exchange, very much as equals, and that God would see things his way and call off the trial. He believed that God would "put strength in him." In other words, Job expected to tell God why it was wrong for him to be going through these trials, and he expected God to say, "You're right, Job, I get it now. Be encouraged, we're all good here!"

Now, please understand, Job was indeed righteous, God said so Himself. And yet, Job's view of this was still very much in error, not because he misunderstood his own greatness, but because he misunderstood how unfathomably great God is. Not to get too far ahead of ourselves, but look at how things went when Job finally got his wish:

Job 42:5 *I have heard of thee by the hearing of the ear: but now mine eye seeth thee. 6 Wherefore I abhor myself, and repent in dust and ashes.*

Pretty different from what Job expected, isn't it! Again, all through this trial, Job understood himself extremely well. But there is no way a finite human being can ever fully grasp God. Because of that, it is wise not to be so brash as to put words in His mouth!

If you ever say, "God said," the next words out of your mouth need to be a Bible verse. Otherwise, DO refrain from putting words in His mouth. If even someone like Job got embarrassed trying that, how much worse off would we be trying that!

Personal Notes:

_____
_____
_____
_____
_____
_____
_____
_____
_____
_____
_____
_____
_____
_____
_____
_____
_____
_____

Devotion 73

Job will do much better in the next few verses. In fact, he will actually give a few simple words that are so rich that even today they are the subject of Christian songs.

Job 23:8 *Behold, I go forward, but he is not there; and backward, but I cannot perceive him:* **9** *On the left hand, where he doth work, but I cannot behold him: he hideth himself on the right hand, that I cannot see him:* **10** *But he knoweth the way that I take: when he hath tried me, I shall come forth as gold.*

Verses eight and nine show Job picturing himself as examining every point of the compass in a desperate attempt to find God and yet failing to do so. He pictures God as hiding Himself in Job's moment of need. And there is more to that than some may realize! Even Jesus looked to heaven in His moment of greatest trial and cried, "My God, my God, why hast thou forsaken me?" Like it or not, the God who has a plan for our lives, a plan to conform us into His image, often uses moments of silence to accomplish that purpose.

But in verse ten, Job uttered the immortal words, "*When he hath tried me, I shall come forth as gold.*" But do you realize what that means? Job was inadvertently stipulating to the fact that even when you cannot seem to find God, God is still actively working in your life! He is burning away the dross, refining the gold, and making something precious out of you.

On the days when you cannot seem to find God, DO remember this phrase, "Maybe I can't find God, but God has never lost sight of me!"

Personal Notes:

Devotion 74

Job, for all that he gets right about God, truly gets one thing wrong about him on a pretty consistent basis.

Job 23:11 *My foot hath held his steps, his way have I kept, and not declined.* **12** *Neither have I gone back from the commandment of his lips; I have esteemed the words of his mouth more than my necessary food.* **13** *But he is in one mind, and who can turn him? and what his soul desireth, even that he doeth.* **14** *For he performeth the thing that is appointed for me: and many such things are with him.* **15** *Therefore am I troubled at his presence: when I consider, I am afraid of him.* **16** *For God maketh my heart soft, and the Almighty troubleth me:* **17** *Because I was not cut off before the darkness, neither hath he covered the darkness from my face.*

Job believed that even if a person always did right in God's sight, God may still arbitrarily pick him out to be angry at and to bring to ruin. He used the word "appointed," meaning that in Job's mind, God predetermined all of this, and nothing Job did could alter the outcome in any way. No wonder Job said, "I am troubled at his presence: when I consider, I am afraid of him!" If a person believes like Job in this, they should be afraid!

But God is not like that. We have what Job did not have–the Bible. We can look from cover to cover and see that God is merciful, loving, and kind. We can also see countless examples of God giving people the "if/then" promise, "If you do right, then I will bless you." We can also see countless examples of God determining to judge people and then changing course when they repented and humbled themselves.

DO remember that this existence, this life, is not a puppet show. God is calling your name, not pulling your strings!

Personal Notes:

_____

_____

_____

_____

_____

_____

_____

_____

_____

_____

_____

_____

_____

_____

_____

_____

_____

_____

_____

_____

_____

_____

_____

_____

Devotion 75

Job's attackers had continually asserted that God always and openly punishes the wicked. Job has repeatedly pushed back against that notion and now does so yet again.

Job 24:1 *Why, seeing times are not hidden from the Almighty, do they that know him not see his days?*

In context, it is times of sin and days of judgment being spoken of. Job was asking why, since God sees all the times the wicked do wrong, do the righteous not get to see Him judging them? Job then introduces a pronoun that he is utterly fixated on, one that we often get fixated on as well.

Job 24:2 *Some remove the landmarks; THEY violently take away flocks, and feed thereof.*

They. In verses two through ten, he will use that pronoun twelve times of the wicked! He says "They take, they drive away, they take, they turn, they go forth, they reap, they gather, they cause, they are, they cause, they pluck, they take."

We often observe that people have "I" trouble, but Job had something nearly as bad, "they" trouble! For a person to spend that much time looking into the lives of others is simply never a good thing, whether you are looking to criticize or looking to be jealous of. Yes, he was correct that the wicked often go unpunished for long years in this life, but it was still incredibly unhealthy of him to have such a fixation on "they!" Job did not realize it, but he was only adding to his misery by peering into the lives of others and wondering why they were doing better than he was.

If you want to be happy, don't spend much time looking at they, or even at I. DO instead spend much time looking at HIM!

Personal Notes:

_____

_____

_____

_____

_____

_____

_____

_____

_____

_____

_____

_____

_____

_____

_____

_____

_____

_____

_____

_____

_____

_____

_____

_____

_____

_____

_____

Devotion 76

Still very much fixated on "they," the wicked, Job turns his attention once again to how they treat others and how it seems that God does not care.

Job 24:12 *Men groan from out of the city, and the soul of the wounded crieth out: yet God layeth not folly to them.*

This is directly contrary to the view of Job's three assailants. They believed that God certainly did lay folly to them. And in a few verses, we will see the main source of this discrepancy in views. But before we get to that, Job deals with a matter of light and darkness, namely the completely accurate view that the wicked hate the light, preferring to commit their heinous acts in the darkness.

Job 24:15 *The eye also of the adulterer waiteth for the twilight, saying, No eye shall see me: and disguiseth his face.* **16** *In the dark they dig through houses, which they had marked for themselves in the daytime: they know not the light.*

Those words are as accurate today as they were 3,500 years ago. The adulterer does prefer the cover of darkness, and thieves do case houses during the day so they can come back late at night and rob them. But that brings us to the crux of the discrepancy, namely a matter of timing.

Job 24:19 *Drought and heat consume the snow waters: so doth the grave those which have sinned.*

Simply put, Job's antagonists believed that God judges people in this life, and Job believed that God judges people by the grave and beyond the grave. And if you know your Bible, you now know the problem, namely that both Job and the Corrosive

Comforters were putting God in a box! God can and often does lower the hammer on the wicked now, and that same God can and often does wait until the grave or the judgment to drop the hammer on the wicked.

Do you hate being frustrated? Then DO let God be what He is, rather than what you demand that He be!

Personal Notes:

_____

_____

_____

_____

_____

_____

_____

_____

_____

_____

_____

_____

_____

_____

_____

_____

_____

_____

_____

_____

_____

_____

_____

Devotion 77

Job and his friends had battled for hour after hour over whether or not the wicked could ever be prosperous in this life and the righteous could ever be impoverished in this life. Job clearly and rightly believed that both of those things were often the case, especially the case of the wicked being prosperous in this life. And in Job 9:21-24 Job gives several concrete examples of the wicked doing wrong and yet prospering until he reached the grave. Having done so, in verse twenty-five, he utters this challenge, "*And if it be not so now, who will make me a liar, and make my speech nothing worth?*" This was a very logical and reasonable demand of Job. "Just give evidence to prove your point or to disapprove mine." And again, the subject was whether or not the wicked ever prosper in this life.

But look at how Bildad answered:

Job 25:2 *Dominion and fear are with him, he maketh peace in his high places. 3 Is there any number of his armies? and upon whom doth not his light arise? 4 How then can man be justified with God? or how can he be clean that is born of a woman? 5 Behold even to the moon, and it shineth not; yea, the stars are not pure in his sight. 6 How much less man, that is a worm? and the son of man, which is a worm?*

If you are a bit confused and scratching your head right now, you have every right to be. Job asked for evidence on a very concrete subject, and Bildad rattled off eighty-three straight words that had literally nothing to do with anything Job said. It is a wonder that Job did not end up with a mug shot for attempted strangulation at this point.

When we are disagreeing with anyone on anything, manners and logic indicate that we answer any honest, direct questions with honest, direct answers. Job was not trying to "gotcha" Bildad, he just wanted to make him understand. But a person more intent on being proven right than finding out what is right will most always handle things wrong.

DO answer honest questions honestly!

Personal Notes:

_____

_____

_____

_____

_____

_____

_____

_____

_____

_____

_____

_____

_____

_____

_____

_____

_____

_____

_____

_____

_____

Devotion 78

As chapter twenty-six begins, Job has finally had enough. He will speak without interruption for six straight chapters; Eliphaz, Bildad, and Zophar will not be heard from again throughout the rest of the book. In our vernacular, we would say Job finally "went off on them." Twice in these chapters, his whole speech here will be called a parable, meaning, in this case, a lengthy proverb designed to impart wisdom. And it is an accurate description because Job, in this proverb/tirade, gives us some of the most magnificent and instructive words in the Bible.

He begins, though, with three verses positively dripping with sarcasm.

Job 26:2 *How hast thou helped him that is without power? how savest thou the arm that hath no strength? 3 How hast thou counselled him that hath no wisdom? and how hast thou plentifully declared the thing as it is? 4 To whom hast thou uttered words? and whose spirit came from thee?*

Bildad's last little speech was designed to impress his hearers with his intellect and understanding. To say the least, he thought way more of himself than others did, especially Job. Job's words in verses two and three basically mean, "exactly how much good do you think you have done here?" with the understood answer being "absolutely none." "To whom hast thou uttered words" means something like, "You are talking to someone with a much higher IQ than your own." And "Whose spirit came from thee?" means something like "I don't know if you think it is God speaking through you or some spirit of wisdom speaking through you, but you should have checked their ID because it is neither."

I will leave it to you to decide whether Job was somehow ungodly in being so sarcastic. What is not up for debate, though, is that Bildad deserved it. No doubt he got very offended by Job's taunts, he probably even filed a grievance with the local Patriarchs Union, but he deserved every bit of this and more.

When you constantly bash others, DO refrain from being surprised or offended when they finally give it right back to you!

Personal Notes:

_____
_____
_____
_____
_____
_____
_____
_____
_____
_____
_____
_____
_____
_____
_____
_____
_____
_____
_____
_____

Devotion 79

Having quickly quieted Bildad with his sarcastic salvo, Job now moves on to discuss God and His greatness. Job's three attackers had pontificated about God's greatness for the purpose of proving that they knew more than he did and that he, therefore, should agree with them. So Job will now demonstrate that he knows more of God's greatness and glory than they do. And in his lengthy lecture on the topic, he really does lay out a ton of treasure for us to consider.

Job 26:5 *Dead things are formed from under the waters, and the inhabitants thereof.* **6** *Hell is naked before him, and destruction hath no covering.*

These two verses are a description of the underworld, hades, hell. Job understood that though humanity could not see into that place, God sees it all.

Job 26:7 *He stretcheth out the north over the empty place, and hangeth the earth upon nothing.*

Job here shows a good understanding of God's creation, and thousands of years before there was such a thing as telescopes. He knew that the northern sky was stretched out over a barren northern land. He knew that the earth was not resting on the back of a giant or riding on the back of a turtle, but was hanging in space on absolutely nothing.

Job 26:13a *By his spirit he hath garnished the heavens; his hand hath formed the crooked serpent.*

Here Job shows an understanding of the fact that there were heavens, plural, meaning our atmosphere, outer space beyond our atmosphere, and the place of God's abode. He knew that God had garnished the heavens, meaning He put all of the heavenly bodies in their place as decorations. He also knew the God who made this massive universe also made all of the tiny creatures on this little speck of dust called earth in that massive universe.

It is clear that, whatever else he may have gotten wrong, Job got it right when it came to the glory of creation and the glory of the God who created it. DO always get those right as well!

Personal Notes:

_____

_____

_____

_____

_____

_____

_____

_____

_____

_____

_____

_____

_____

_____

_____

_____

_____

_____

_____

_____

_____

_____

Devotion 80

Continuing his speech on into chapter twenty-seven, Job once again turns his attention to the immediate issue at hand, his suffering, and his friends' accusations because of that suffering.

Job 27:1 *Moreover Job continued his parable, and said, 2 As God liveth, who hath taken away my judgment; and the Almighty, who hath vexed my soul; 3 All the while my breath is in me, and the spirit of God is in my nostrils; 4 My lips shall not speak wickedness, nor my tongue utter deceit. 5 God forbid that I should justify you: till I die I will not remove mine integrity from me.*

As he has done repeatedly, Job once again makes a mistake in verse two of believing that it is God who has ruined him. Nonetheless, he was right in his assertion that in order to agree with his friends, he would have to lie to do it. And he absolutely, as he should have, refused to ever do that.

Job's attackers had literally put him in a place where he would have to sin in order to agree that he had sinned, and if he didn't, his friends would regard him as a sinner. Talk about a no-win situation! Mind you, this was not a matter of Job agreeing that at some point he had sinned; Job would absolutely have agreed with that. This was a matter of Job being accused of everything from child abuse, to theft from widows, and much more, and that being the reason he was experiencing such tragedy. Job knew that none of that was true, and no amount of badgering was going to get him to break, no matter how hard officers Bildad, Zophar, and Eliphaz tried to squeeze a lawyerless confession out of Job.

As crazy as it sounds, you will meet people in life who are very easy to get along with; all you have to do is agree with their evaluation of you, no matter how far off base it is. But lying is still a sin, and it is better to be right with God than right with man.

If you ever meet such obnoxious people, DO be honest about yourself, even if that means saying, "I am in the right on this one, and I won't back down!"

Personal Notes:

_____

_____

_____

_____

_____

_____

_____

_____

_____

_____

_____

_____

_____

_____

_____

_____

_____

_____

_____

_____

Devotion 81

Continuing on in his heated, multi-chapter closing monologue against his attackers, Job will once again distinguish himself from the wicked and remind his estranged friends that they have seen the proof of his claims.

Job 27:6 *My righteousness I hold fast, and will not let it go: my heart shall not reproach me so long as I live.* **7** *Let mine enemy be as the wicked, and he that riseth up against me as the unrighteous.* **8** *For what is the hope of the hypocrite, though he hath gained, when God taketh away his soul?* **9** *Will God hear his cry when trouble cometh upon him?* **10** *Will he delight himself in the Almighty? will he always call upon God?* **11** *I will teach you by the hand of God: that which is with the Almighty will I not conceal.* **12** *Behold, all ye yourselves have seen it; why then are ye thus altogether vain?*

Job's appeal in verse twelve was for his attackers to simply acknowledge what they themselves had seen with their own eyes in his life. They had known him for years, they had never had a single doubt about his righteousness, and yet they were now proclaiming that he was unrighteous the entire time. Little wonder, then, that Job said, "*Why then are ye thus altogether vain?*" meaning, "Why are you such lightweights, so empty of substance?"

It was a fair criticism. Either they had been completely wrong about him for years, or they were completely wrong about him now. And yet they were acting as if they were the wisest people around and that Job should simply agree with them even though they were contradicting everything they used to say and believe.

That is generally a sign of a person who should not be taken seriously. If a person bounces back and forth between radically differing opinions and yet still regards himself as the smartest person in the room, DO know that the only way that is possible is if he is the only person in the room!

Personal Notes:

_____

_____

_____

_____

_____

_____

_____

_____

_____

_____

_____

_____

_____

_____

_____

_____

_____

_____

_____

_____

_____

Devotion 82

For the remainder of chapter twenty-seven, Job once again reiterated his belief that the wicked are judged by God after their death and that such judgment even affects their descendants. But as chapter twenty-eight begins, Job will give a lengthy description of the industry of man. He is not changing subjects, he is beginning to paint a word picture to demonstrate a point.

Job 28:1 *Surely there is a vein for the silver, and a place for gold where they fine it.* **2** *Iron is taken out of the earth, and brass is molten out of the stone.*

Please remember that we are talking about mankind from nearly 4,000 years ago. They had no electric tools, no internal combustion engines, no heavy equipment. And yet they learned that silver runs in veins and how to get it. They learned how to get gold out of the earth and refine it. They learned how to get and produce iron and how to smelt brass. And, continuing that thought through verse eleven, he shows man searching the depths of the earth for precious stones, rerouting rivers, and digging into things so deep that it is as if he has dug up the very shadow of death. Man is an explorer, and even with merely primitive tools, he can very nearly do the impossible.

But here is the point of all that Job said:

Job 28:12 *But where shall wisdom be found? and where is the place of understanding?*

Job was not inferring that wisdom can never be found, for he himself claimed to have it multiple times throughout the book. He was, though, saying that while there is nothing on earth that man cannot uncover and discover, there are parts of wisdom and understanding that will always be beyond his reach. He was telling his adversaries, again, that they needed to stop acting like know-it-alls.

DO strive for wisdom and understanding in every thing, every day. But DO also have enough humility to realize that you will never know it all on this side of heaven!

Personal Notes:

_____

_____

_____

_____

_____

_____

_____

_____

_____

_____

_____

_____

_____

_____

_____

_____

_____

_____

_____

_____

_____

Devotion 83

Job began chapter twenty-eight describing how man digs down the earth looking for gold and silver and precious jewels and other valuable substances. He then applied that picture in pointing out that while all those things could not be hidden from man, much of wisdom will always be hidden from man no matter how deep we dig for it. Now, in verses thirteen through nineteen, he will describe the value of wisdom.

Job 28:13 *Man knoweth not the price thereof; neither is it found in the land of the living.* **14** *The depth saith, It is not in me: and the sea saith, It is not with me.* **15** *It cannot be gotten for gold, neither shall silver be weighed for the price thereof.* **16** *It cannot be valued with the gold of Ophir, with the precious onyx, or the sapphire.* **17** *The gold and the crystal cannot equal it: and the exchange of it shall not be for jewels of fine gold.* **18** *No mention shall be made of coral, or of pearls: for the price of wisdom is above rubies.* **19** *The topaz of Ethiopia shall not equal it, neither shall it be valued with pure gold.*

Job mentions gold five times, then also mentions silver, onyx, sapphire, crystal, jewels, coral, pearls, rubies, and topaz. None of these things can buy wisdom, even if you put them all together!

So, are you thoroughly discouraged now, as you seek for wisdom in your life? Don't be. In the next devotion and in the next few verses, Job will begin to hint at how to attain that precious thing that cannot be bought. But for now, just take note of how incredibly valuable wisdom is! In general, people jump at the chance to gain things like gold and silver and precious jewels, people have their hearts set on money and riches. But wisdom is more valuable by far!

DO set your heart on wisdom. People who are dumb and rich generally end up just being dumb; people who are wise are eternally rich even if they don't have a dime in their pockets!

Personal Notes:

_____

_____

_____

_____

_____

_____

_____

_____

_____

_____

_____

_____

_____

_____

_____

_____

_____

_____

_____

_____

_____

_____

Devotion 84

Job just spent several verses proving that wisdom cannot be bought. And, while anyone in our day who has seen people spend a quarter million dollars on an Ivy League education in gender studies already knows that, it was a bit of a shocking truth to those in Job's day. But now he will tell us where wisdom can be gotten.

Job 28:23 *God understandeth the way thereof, and he knoweth the place thereof.*

We find, then, that wisdom is found in a person, God, not a place, the ground. And that God has been kind enough to give us some instructions on the matter:

Job 28:28 *And unto man he said, Behold, the fear of the Lord, that is wisdom; and to depart from evil is understanding.*

That is the foundational truth about wisdom. Solomon would reiterate it thousands of years later in Proverbs 1:7. We can dig into the ground for an entire lifetime and get only dumber and dirtier. But a person who spends a lifetime digging into God always gets wiser.

DO open your own personal "God Mine" and dig into it every day!

Personal Notes:

_____
_____
_____
_____
_____
_____
_____
_____
_____
_____
_____
_____
_____
_____
_____
_____
_____
_____
_____
_____
_____
_____
_____
_____
_____
_____
_____
_____

Devotion 85

Job 29 gives us the largest window and clearest view into Job's life previous to his calamities. Reading it, it is no wonder Job was so mournful; if ever a man had a storybook life, Job did. We will spend a few devotions looking at it in sections.

Job 29:1 *Moreover Job continued his parable, and said,* **2** *Oh that I were as in months past, as in the days when God preserved me;* **3** *When his candle shined upon my head, and when by his light I walked through darkness;* **4** *As I was in the days of my youth, when the secret of God was upon my tabernacle;* **5** *When the Almighty was yet with me, when my children were about me;* **6** *When I washed my steps with butter, and the rock poured me out rivers of oil;*

Verses two through four show us the closeness that Job felt to God. From his youth on, God preserved him, gave him light, and seemed to reveal precious secrets to him. Verse five reminds us that Job did not just have children, he had children who were close to him, children who adored him. Verse six is a picturesque description of his wealth. Anyone who can afford to wash his steps with butter, anyone to who it seems the very rocks are pouring out precious olive oil, is a wealthy man.

Job missed all of that. He mourned for it, and who can blame him? But do you see the flip side of that coin? The reason Job could be so heartbroken over all he had lost is because he had it all to lose! The devil did not show up in heaven and say, "Job can't even afford to pay attention, but give me a chance and I'm sure I can find something to take from him!" No, the second most powerful being in the universe had noticed his blessings.

Loss is very hard to deal with, for anyone. But when it comes, DO remember that the reason you can feel such pain is because God gave you so many blessings to begin with!

Personal Notes:

_____

_____

_____

_____

_____

_____

_____

_____

_____

_____

_____

_____

_____

_____

_____

_____

_____

_____

_____

_____

_____

_____

_____

Devotion 86

Continuing on in his description of his wonderful days prior to Satan attacking him, Job will use verses seven through seventeen to show his official office in his society.

Job 29:7 *When I went out to the gate through the city, when I prepared my seat in the street!* **8** *The young men saw me, and hid themselves: and the aged arose, and stood up.* **9** *The princes refrained talking, and laid their hand on their mouth.* **10** *The nobles held their peace, and their tongue cleaved to the roof of their mouth.* **11** *When the ear heard me, then it blessed me; and when the eye saw me, it gave witness to me:* **12** *Because I delivered the poor that cried, and the fatherless, and him that had none to help him.* **13** *The blessing of him that was ready to perish came upon me: and I caused the widow's heart to sing for joy.* **14** *I put on righteousness, and it clothed me: my judgment was as a robe and a diadem.* **15** *I was eyes to the blind, and feet was I to the lame.* **16** *I was a father to the poor: and the cause which I knew not I searched out.* **17** *And I brake the jaws of the wicked, and plucked the spoil out of his teeth.*

This is a clear description of a judge. Job was so venerable that people allowed him to mediate their disputes, and he did a good job of it. Young men were awed by him, old men stood up to honor him, and rulers fell silent in his presence. Job used his position to take care of the poor, the fatherless, the widow, and the handicapped. He also was the wicked man's worst nightmare. Wouldn't you love to have judges like that today!

And yet, even if you never have an earthly judge like that, you can BE an earthly judge like that in any matters and disputes that are before you. You can make a difference, and if you do, you, like Job, will never forget it.

DO make a difference!

Personal Notes:

_____

_____

_____

_____

_____

_____

_____

_____

_____

_____

_____

_____

_____

_____

_____

_____

_____

_____

_____

_____

_____

_____

_____

_____

Devotion 87

Job will use the third section of chapter twenty-nine to give us his general emotional state and thought process before his world fell apart.

Job 29:18 *Then I said, I shall die in my nest, and I shall multiply my days as the sand.* **19** *My root was spread out by the waters, and the dew lay all night upon my branch.* **20** *My glory was fresh in me, and my bow was renewed in my hand.* **21** *Unto me men gave ear, and waited, and kept silence at my counsel.* **22** *After my words they spake not again; and my speech dropped upon them.* **23** *And they waited for me as for the rain; and they opened their mouth wide as for the latter rain.* **24** *If I laughed on them, they believed it not; and the light of my countenance they cast not down.* **25** *I chose out their way, and sat chief, and dwelt as a king in the army, as one that comforteth the mourners.*

Simply put, Job was regarded as royalty and drew a great deal of pleasure from it. Who wouldn't? He felt calm, safe, secure, and for the most part, he was anxiety-free. He had no real people problems; everyone sought his favor. So again, Job had a lot to lose.

And he lost it. He lost not just the material blessings, his health, and his family, but he lost his peace of mind as well. And even if he had lost nothing else, that by itself is enormous. Sometimes, people seem to be in good circumstances, but their peace of mind has, for some reason, been shattered.

DO show compassion to those people; if it rattled Job, it would rattle any of us!

Personal Notes:

_____
_____
_____
_____
_____
_____
_____
_____
_____
_____
_____
_____
_____
_____
_____
_____
_____
_____
_____
_____
_____
_____
_____

Devotion 88

Job had spoken of his glory at the end of chapter twenty-nine and, specifically, of his glory before man. He was a very well-respected individual before all of his calamity. But as he begins chapter thirty, he quickly tells us just how drastically things had changed for him.

Job 30:1 *But now they that are younger than I have me in derision, whose fathers I would have disdained to have set with the dogs of my flock.*

This is a very harsh statement from Job, and it is harsh by design. Job is pointing out that it is not just young people in general mocking him for no reason that he has a problem with; young people whose fathers were the very dregs of society, people not even fit to watch the dogs who watched the sheep, even those young people now held him in derision. And, lest you bristle at that and regard it as unspiritual of Job, may I ask you this question? If you have dogs, are there some people that you would not trust them with?

Unless there is something fairly odd about you, I am quite certain that the answer is yes. There are people who are so disreputable and dishonest and vile that we would not trust any of our animals with, let alone our home or our children. Job goes on in verses two through eight to describe these people at length, pointing out that they were weak (v.2), destitute and timid (v.3), impoverished (v.4), skulking (v.5-6), acted like donkeys (v.7), and the traits of their entire families were foolish, base, and vile (v.8).

In other words, they were people who should have been way too aware of their own huge shortcomings to ever mock anyone else! And yet, finding Job in such a weakened state, they attacked him like a pack of wild animals.

We cannot go back in time and protect Job from those people/animals. But we can teach our own children to never be like that. Imagine how different things would have been if parents had ever taught these children to simply be nice! So DO teach your children that lesson often, and early!

Personal Notes:

_____

_____

_____

_____

_____

_____

_____

_____

_____

_____

_____

_____

_____

_____

_____

_____

_____

_____

_____

_____

Devotion 89

As Job continues to lament the degrading way he is now treated by young people who used to stand in awe of him, we find both some horrible cruelty and also what Job believed to be the root of the problem.

Job 30:9 *And now am I their song, yea, I am their byword.* **10** *They abhor me, they flee far from me, and spare not to spit in my face.* **11** *Because he hath loosed my cord, and afflicted me, they have also let loose the bridle before me.* **12** *Upon my right hand rise the youth; they push away my feet, and they raise up against me the ways of their destruction.* **13** *They mar my path, they set forward my calamity, they have no helper.* **14** *They came upon me as a wide breaking in of waters: in the desolation they rolled themselves upon me.*

The song that Job spoke of in verse nine was a song of taunting, not a song of encouragement. And the fact that he was a byword means that those young people were using his very name as if it were an insult. In verse ten, we find that not only did they abhor Job and abandon him whenever he called for help, they also, when they did come near, actually spit in his face. Can you imagine people ever being so horrible? All the way through verse fourteen, Job continues to list the details of the terrible way they treated him.

But it is in verse eleven that we find what Job believed to be the problem. He said, "*Because he* [God] *hath loosed my cord, and afflicted me, they* [those cruel youth] *have also let loose the bridle before me.*" The picture of the loosing of the cord was that of a bow that had been unstrung and was no longer dangerous and powerful. Seeing Job in that condition, those kids "let loose the bridle," meaning they threw off any restraints of how they treated Job.

Job thought, again, that God had done this to him. But his error in this is not what I am focused on. My attention is drawn to the fact that there are people who are only kind when it benefits them, meaning they are not really kind at all. These kids had once treated Job right, but only as long as Job was healthy and whole and powerful. Their entire behavior changed once there was no more benefit to being kind.

When it benefits you to be kind, DO be kind. When it does not benefit you to be kind, DO be kind. If you are only kind when it benefits you, you are not really kind at all!

Personal Notes:

_____

_____

_____

_____

_____

_____

_____

_____

_____

_____

_____

_____

_____

_____

_____

_____

Devotion 90

In verses sixteen through eighteen, Job leaves off the subject of his young tormentors and returns to the oft-mentioned subject of his wrecked physical and emotional condition.

Job 30:16 *And now my soul is poured out upon me; the days of affliction have taken hold upon me.* **17** *My bones are pierced in me in the night season: and my sinews take no rest.* **18** *By the great force of my disease is my garment changed: it bindeth me about as the collar of my coat.*

Job was empty inside; he said, "*My soul is poured out upon me.*" He felt trapped; he said, "*The days of affliction have taken hold upon me.*" When he tried to sleep, it felt like his bones had nails run through them, and his sinews, his muscles and connective tissues, could not get any rest. But verse eighteen is the most gruesome description of all, and it sheds some real light on the sufferings of Job and on why anyone in their right mind would have shown him pity. He said, "*By the great force of my disease is my garment changed: it bindeth me about as the collar of my coat.*" In other words, his skin had become like some mangled animal hide, it had enveloped his body as if it were a garment, and he could not get out. Think "the Elephant Man," only far worse.

That sort of changes our picture of things, doesn't it? Somehow, we normally seem to view the situation as one in which Job's three friends/attackers sat across from him, and all four of them looked a lot alike, except for Job having some sores on him. And nothing could be farther from the truth. Job barely looked human, if at all, and everyone knew there was no medical cure for his condition.

This is what the devil did to Job. But before God lowered the hedge that Satan complained about in Job 1:10, he could do none of this! So, on the days when you feel like you have nothing to be thankful for, look in the mirror at the normal human skin on your body, and DO thank God for that divine hedge of protection that God maintains about you!

Personal Notes:

_____

_____

_____

_____

_____

_____

_____

_____

_____

_____

_____

_____

_____

_____

_____

_____

_____

_____

_____

Devotion 91

In verses twenty-five through twenty-eight, Job looks back in time to his behavior and to what he expected based on that behavior. He then brings up an issue of worship.

Job 30:25 *Did not I weep for him that was in trouble? was not my soul grieved for the poor?* **26** *When I looked for good, then evil came unto me: and when I waited for light, there came darkness.* **27** *My bowels boiled, and rested not: the days of affliction prevented me.* **28** *I went mourning without the sun: I stood up, and I cried in the congregation.*

As he has reiterated throughout the book, Job had been very attentive to the needs of others. His heart empathized with anyone in difficulty. And he knew that God approved of that. And that is what surprised him so badly; verse twenty-six says, "*When I looked for good, then evil came unto me: and when I waited for light, there came darkness.*"

Job understood the law of sowing and reaping. What he did not understand was why it did not seem to be working! We often have the same issue and for the same reason; timing. Yes, we do reap what we sow, but the "when" is often nowhere near as soon as we would like!

But it is verse twenty-eight that captivates me at the moment, specifically Job's statement that he stood up, and cried in the congregation. Sometime after his calamity began, Job went to worship. But as he stood up, all he could do was cry. I wager to say that every child of God has been there at some point or other.

But he went. Pain and all, he went. Emotional turmoil and all, he went. Knowing he was going to shed tears, he went.

He went.

DO be as faithful as Job; God is just as moved by the tears of a worshipper as He is by the triumphant testimony of a worshipper!

Personal Notes:

_____

_____

_____

_____

_____

_____

_____

_____

_____

_____

_____

_____

_____

_____

_____

_____

_____

_____

_____

_____

_____

_____

_____

_____

_____

Devotion 92

Job will now close out chapter thirty with another picturesque description of his calamity.

Job 30:29 *I am a brother to dragons, and a companion to owls.* **30** *My skin is black upon me, and my bones are burned with heat.* **31** *My harp also is turned to mourning, and my organ into the voice of them that weep.*

Whatever the Bible meant when it described dragons, they were clearly a solitary, isolated creature, as were the owls of the night. Job, who had once been the toast of the town, now was like Beauty's beast in the desolate castle, just waiting to die alone. And his skin, which a few verses earlier we noted had become like an elephant hide engulfing his body, had turned a diseased black. His bones felt like they were on fire. His voice, which had once been melodious, was now raspy with mourning and weeping.

And yet, through all of the negative descriptions, two words stick out to me: brother and companion. Job was not a "solitary dragon;" he was a brother to dragons. He was not a solitary owl; he was a companion to owls. In other words, somewhere along the line, there were other hurting people that Job was aware of and had somehow drawn strength from!

And isn't that just the way God works? Even in our times of greatest darkness, it seems that God tends to bring along others who know that darkness well so that we are never quite completely alone.

So, dear hurting dragon or withdrawn owl, DO look around and realize that you may not have everyone you want gathered around you, but you do at least have a few that you need!

Personal Notes:

_____

_____

_____

_____

_____

_____

_____

_____

_____

_____

_____

_____

_____

_____

_____

_____

_____

_____

_____

_____

_____

_____

_____

_____

Devotionals

DO Drops Volume 1
DO Drops Volume 2
DO Drops Volume 3
DO Drops Volume 4
DO Drops Volume 5
DO Drops Volume 6
DO Drops Volume 7
DO Drops Volume 8
DO Drops Volume 9
DO Drops Volume 10
DO Drops Volume 11

More Books by Dr. Bo Wagner

Beyond the Colored Coat
Don't Muzzle the Ox
From Footers to Finish Nails
I'm Saved! Now What???
Learning Not to Fear the Old Testament
Marriage Makers/Marriage Breakers
Daniel: Breathtaking
Esther: Five Feast and the Fingerprints of God
Ephesians: Treasures of Family
Galatians: Treasures of Liberty
James: The Pen and the Plumb Line
Jonah: A Study in Greatness
Nehemiah: A Labor of Love
Proverbs: Bright Lights from Dark Sayings Vol 1
Proverbs: Bright Lights from Dark Sayings Vol 2
Romans: Salvation From A-Z
Ruth: Diamonds in the Darkness
The Revelation: Ready or Not

Books in the Night Heroes Series

Cry From the Coal Mine (Vol. 1)
Free Fall (Vol. 2)
Broken Brotherhood (Vol. 3)
The Blade of Black Crow (Vol. 4)
Ghost Ship (Vol. 5)
When Serpents Rise (Vol. 6)
Moth Man (Vol. 7)
Runaway (Vol. 8)
Terror by Day (Vol. 9)
Winter Wolf (Vol. 10)
Desert Heat (Vol. 11)

Sci-Fi

Zak Blue and the Great Space Chase Series:
Falcon Wing (Vol. 1)
Enter the Maelstrom (Vol. 2)

www.ingramcontent.com/pod-product-compliance
Lightning Source LLC
Chambersburg PA
CBHW072003040426
42447CB00009B/1473